Children and Prejudice

Social Psychology and Society

General Editors: Howard Giles and Miles Hewstone

Children and Prejudice

Frances Aboud

Basil Blackwell

Copyright © Frances Aboud 1988

First published 1988

Basil Blackwell Ltd
108 Cowley Road, Oxford, OX4 1JF, UK

Basil Blackwell Inc.
432 Park Avenue South, Suite 1503
New York, NY 10016, USA

British Library Cataloguing in Publication Data

Aboud, Frances
    Children and prejudice—(Social psychology and society).
    1. Race awareness in children
    I. Title   II. Series
    305.23   BF723.R3

    ISBN 0–631–14939–2
    ISBN 0–631–14941–4 Pbk

Library of Congress Cataloging in Publication Data

Aboud, Frances E.
    Children and prejudice.
    (Social psychology and society)
    Includes index.
    1. Prejudices in children.   2. Ethnicity in children.
    3. Race awareness in children.
    I. Title.   II. Series.
    BF723.P75A24 1988   305.2′3   87–31472

    ISBN 0–631–14939–2
    ISBN 0–631–14941–4 (pbk.)

Typeset by Columns of Reading
Printed in the USA

Contents

To my husband Charles
and two wonderful children Charles and Leila

Editors' Preface

One of the most depressing aspects of prejudice is the early age at which it rears its ugly head. The developmental psychological literature on this topic is replete with tragi-comic examples of how young children think and talk about race. A little black girl says to her white friend, 'I'd hate to be coloured, wouldn't you?'; a small white boy refuses to sit next to a black doll claiming, 'If I have to sit next to one of those – I'll have a nervous breakdown.' Such examples (taken from research) embarrass parents, frustrate teachers and intrigue researchers.

In this second volume of the series, *Social Psychology and Society*, Frances Aboud delivers an accessible and important message to educators, researchers and interested members of the general public. She cuts through a mass of evidence to provide clear conclusions on a topic riddled with complexities and contradictions. Herein, conclusions are succinctly stated in the summaries at the ends of each chapter. For example, when are ethnic attitudes first acquired? (around the age of 4 years); at what age are children aware of different ethnic groups? (4–5 years).

The most original and provocative aspect of this book is its new 'social-cognitive developmental' theory of prejudice. Aboud argues that because of their cognitive limitations, children are almost inevitably prejudiced up to the age of about 7 years. Further, prejudice is not solely a relationship between parents' and children's attitudes. This is, in fact, an optimistic perspective, which argues strongly for active educational intervention as children reach that age (about 7) when they are cognitively capable of being less prejudicial. In this way, the author takes the relationship between social psychology and society full circle, feeding back constructive proposals to the classrooms in which prejudice develops and, perhaps, can be thwarted.

Howard Giles and Miles Hewstone

Preface

Prejudice is an electrifying topic that everyone seems to hold an opinion on. Bring up an incident of prejudice at any gathering of people and there are inevitably those who attempt to justify it and those who are indignant. My own opinion is that prejudice is harmful both to those who harbour it and to those who are targeted by it. But another side of me enjoys listening to the arguments put forth by both sides as I try to analyse what lies behind the emotion.

My formal research on ethnic relations began at McGill University while I was a doctoral student working with Donald Taylor, Wally Lambert and Dick Tucker. We approached the study of prejudice, stereotypes and identity from a social psychological perspective. Gradually, the subjects of my investigation became younger and younger. To my surprise, the results of my own and others' research with young children did not fit the descriptions or explanations of adult prejudice proposed by social psychologists. What was missing was an understanding of the social, emotional and cognitive capabilities of children at different ages.

To be fair, developmental psychologists have not until recently been able to provide this understanding. However, in the past decade, research on cognitive and especially social development has increased greatly. It is now possible to understand prejudice in children in the light of other developing cognitive and social skills. This has permitted a new, more child-oriented perspective on the development of prejudice. Prejudice in children can be viewed as not simply a miniature version of adult prejudice, but as a reflection of their age-related level of functioning. Further advances in our understanding of emotional development, which is presently meagre, will inevitably necessitate further revisions in the current perspective.

Many people become interested in the topic of prejudice through personal and professional experience. I have written the book primarily for educators and researchers – people who want to know the current levels and explanations of prejudice (educators), people who want to know how to measure prejudice and design a study (new researchers), and people who want an up-to-date integration of the field and a new theory with hypotheses to test (more sophisticated researchers). The chapters therefore follow a sequence that begins with definitions and measures, followed by theoretical predictions, empirical research, and finally a formulation of the social-cognitive developmental explanation of prejudice.

In writing this book, I received assistance from a number of my students including Shelagh Skerry, Sydney Miller, David Schwartzbein and Louise Chartrand. Sheila Morrin has been a supportive secretary throughout this project. I am also grateful to Mark Zanna, Anna Beth Doyle, Wally Lambert, Miles Hewstone and Howard Giles for commenting on drafts of the chapters. In addition, I would like to acknowledge the strong support I received from the International Association of Cross-Cultural Psychologists and from the Society for Research in Child Development who provided me with the occasions for developing and publicly presenting some of the ideas expressed in this book.

Figure 3 is reprinted with permission of the North-Holland Publishing Company, Amsterdam, from an article by F.E. Aboud and F.G. Mitchell entitled 'Ethnic role-taking: The effects of preference and self-identification', *International Journal of Psychology*, 12, 5. The other figures in the book are reproduced from drawings and photographs which are my own and have not been published before. Table 1, from the *Journal of Genetic Psychology*, 145, 225, is reprinted with permission of the Helen Dwight Reid Educational Foundation. Published by Heldref Publications, 4000 Albemarle St, NW, Washington, DC, 20016. Copyright © 1984.

Frances Aboud
Montreal

1 What Is Prejudice and Ethnic Awareness?

We have all become more aware of the existence of prejudice in our own and other countries. Race riots in the United States and Britain, sanctions against South Africa for its apartheid policy, land claims made by Amerindians for their lost territory, trials against Nazi war criminals, and other events have been brought to our attention by an investigative and inquisitive media. I, for one, thought that this awareness was accompanied by a decline in prejudice. Where once people had without much thought simply accepted the widespread belief that certain ethnic groups were inferior, and had adopted the prejudices and discriminatory practices of their community, they were now more thoughtful about such matters. The awareness of another perspective, the empathy for oppressed groups and the outrage against inequality transformed prejudice from an 'automatic' and mindless reaction to a highly sensitive and salient issue. Now that the issue has become less controversial, many people fear that prejudice is slowly increasing again. Although it is too early to say whether this fear is justified, there is cause for both pessimism and optimism.

Stories in the news as well as opinion polls make it clear that prejudice is still very common in many countries. In a survey conducted for *Time* magazine (2 February 1987 issue), 92 per cent of Blacks and 87 per cent of Whites agreed that 'Racial prejudice is still very common in the US'. Almost an equal percentage, around 40 per cent–50 per cent, of Whites and Blacks felt that prejudice worked in both directions – that most White Americans do not like Blacks and that most Black Americans do not like Whites. Interestingly, 64 per cent of the White respondents but only 30 per cent of the Black respondents said they would be afraid to go into a homogeneous neighbourhood of the other race at night. The statistics are interesting because they run counter to a recent highly publicized incident in which Blacks were attacked in an all-White neighbourhood. In New York City, a group of White youths beat up three Black men, one of whom died as he ran from his attackers and was hit by a car. The incident became a rallying point for many Blacks and Whites, whose aggressive retaliation and expressions of anger and hatred toward the other group went beyond indignation at the incident itself. It is as if these people identified with the attackers or with the victims and felt compelled to replay the incident with their own ending. The incident disinhibited emotions of fear, anger and hatred which had previously been controlled. The fact that prejudices can be triggered in this way brings to light the real possibility that a lot of intense negative feelings remain hidden until brought to the surface by an arousing incident.

Although it is clear that prejudice has not disappeared, most statistics confirm that it has declined since the 1950s (see Rothbart's 1976 review of the US statistics). For example, in 1942 only 21 per cent of Southern US Whites believed that Blacks could be as intelligent as Whites, whereas in 1963, 59 per cent believed this. The figures for Northern US Whites increased from 50 per cent to 84 per cent in the same time period.

In Canada, the authors of a nationwide survey of ethnic attitudes found the climate to be generally positive. People were on the whole favourable toward different ethnic groups, favourable toward immigration, and supportive of the multicultural policy which encourages maintenance of ethnic differences (Berry, Kalin and Taylor, 1976). Despite these positive signs, there were indications that certain groups are evaluated more negatively than others. At the bottom of the ethnic hierarchy were Chinese, Spanish, Greek, Native Indian, Negro and East Indian groups. Furthermore, only 33 per cent of the Canadians surveyed were willing to accept immigrants from communist countries, and only 66 per cent were willing to accept immigrants 'who are coloured'. Thus, we see that though there is less prejudice now than there was 30 and 40 years ago, it has not by any means disappeared.

Most of us think of prejudice as an adolescent or adult phenomenon. If we encounter prejudice in children, we are quick to attribute it to their innocent imitation of adults, rather than to their own personal preferences. This attribution is unjustified according to current research. We cannot truthfully say that prejudice in children simply reflects adult prejudice, and will therefore rise and fall in line with adult levels in the community. In fact, there is good reason to believe that the level of prejudice in children from 4 to 7 years has not declined in the past 40 years as it has in adults (e.g. Clark and Clark, 1947; Greenwald and Oppenheim, 1968; Stevenson and Stewart, 1958). It has remained high despite the dramatic social changes in race relations. It has remained high despite the lower levels of prejudice in their parents.

What accounts for high levels of prejudice in young children if not their parents' attitudes? What is the prognosis for later tolerance given such high levels of prejudice in the early years? Is the prejudice of a child similar to the prejudice of an adult? These are questions that come to mind when one tries to understand the complex connection between childhood and adult prejudice. They are questions that I hope to address in the following chapters.

To answer these questions, one must have a definition of prejudice. Although the definition of prejudice must be the same regardless of the person or age group to whom it applies, prejudiced individuals are not always the same. Lest we fall into the habit of imagining only one type of 'prejudiced person', I would like to describe three of the many types encountered by Adorno, Frenkel–Brunswick, Levinson and Sanford (1950) in their study of the prejudiced adult.

Most prevalent were the conventional and the authoritarian types. Conventionally prejudiced people speak about conforming to the prejudice norms of their group in order to identify with or feel a part of that group. Their prejudice consists of an external set of values that they have adopted from other people. These people are content with their social life and with society. Authoritarian people, in contrast, show a great deal of impulsive anger and aggression along with their prejudices. They hold strongly to their beliefs and emotions, which are often tinged with feelings of revenge. For this reason, their prejudice appears to be more a reflection of internal needs than of social standards. A third, less prevalent type of prejudiced adult is the one whose prejudice reflects their own temporary difficulties in coping with life's challenges. There is no evidence of deep-seated anger, but rather a feeling of frustration with current personal and social problems. The problems and frustrations are in turn blamed on other people, such as parents and outgroups. Although these three types of people are equally prejudiced, they express their prejudice in different ways. They alert us to the possibility that prejudice in children may also vary, not only because of individual differences but also because each age brings with it a different set of personal and social limitations and capabilities.

Most people recognize prejudice when they encounter it – directed at themselves or at someone else. Unfortunately, this has been the source of one major problem in the study of prejudice, namely that researchers opt for a simple and obvious measure of prejudice rather than for one that is conceptually complete or psychometrically sound. Take for example a child's statement that the person shown in a picture is bad. Although this sounds like prejudice, one would want to look more carefully before calling it such. For example, one would want to see if the negative feeling occurred reliably for that child and if it generalized to other people of that ethnic background. Researchers of prejudice have been slow to develop standardized measures and those measures that are standardized are not used frequently enough.

This chapter will begin with a discussion of the psychological definition of prejudice and its major components. Because the awareness of ethnic or racial groups is considered to be a prerequisite for prejudice, it too will be defined and discussed. Awareness of ethnic groups, awareness of one's own ethnicity and prejudice are three ways in which children react to the differences they notice among people. Although the three are inevitably related to one another, they refer to conceptually distinct reactions. The second half of this chapter deals with the ways each has been measured in children. Later chapters will describe the prejudice and ethnic awareness found in children using these measures.

A DEFINITION OF PREJUDICE

The most salient characteristic of prejudice is its negative, hateful quality. This negativity defines prejudice. More precisely, prejudice refers to an organized predisposition to respond in an unfavourable manner toward people from an ethnic group because of their ethnic affiliation. Thus, in addition to making unfavourable or negative judgements, a person must possess two other features if he or she is to be called prejudiced. One is an underlying organized predisposition to feel negatively toward such people. Another is that the negativity be directed toward persons because of their ethnic or racial group membership, and not only because of some individual attribute.

The three components must all be present for us to know that the person is prejudiced. It is somewhat easier to isolate what is meant by discrimination because it refers to overt actions which treat different ethnic groups differently. For prejudice, there must be an unfavourable evaluation of a person, elicited by his/her ethnic group membership, and based on an underlying organized predisposition. A more complete description of each will soon reveal problems in applying this largely adult-oriented definition to children. The problems arise mainly because certain components of the definition are too sophisticated to exist as such in children. For example, the psychological structures of children are generally simpler than those of adults, in the sense of being less differentiated and less integrated. Similarly, we should expect the structure of prejudice to be simpler in children, perhaps less organized and perhaps less categorical when they are very young. It may be useful, therefore, to think of rudimentary forms of a prejudiced attitude, which precede the adult form.

The first and most important indicator of prejudice is a negative evaluation. This may take the form of disliking a person or group of persons, or describing them in negative terms such as bad, ugly, mean or dirty. It is helpful to distinguish conceptually between prejudice and stereotypes even though in reality the two may often occur together. Stereotypes are rigid, overgeneralized beliefs about the attributes of ethnic group members whereas prejudice is a negative attitude. Thus, one may have a stereotype about a group toward whom one is favourable. Moreover, two people may hold the same stereotype but one be prejudiced and the other positive. The distinction is harder to make when the attribute applied to an ethnic group member is clearly evaluative, for example, mean or stupid. To me this reflects prejudice which in turn infuses the stereotype with negative attributes. When the attribute is not evaluative but is applied to all members regardless of their individual qualities, it is a stereotype. For example, statements such as 'Chinese people don't speak English', 'Eskimos eat raw fish' and 'Blacks are poor' may sound prejudicial because they emphasize concrete attributes and because they are overgeneralizations. Nonetheless, they are basically descriptive rather than evaluative. They reflect stereotypes held by the child but not necessarily a prejudicial attitude. An attitude, then, must have an evaluative component. Because preferences, evaluation and affect are clearly present in young children, there is no problem in using this criterion to identify prejudice in children.

The second component is that the evaluation is elicited by the person's ethnicity and not only by the unique, personal qualities of the individual. Prejudice exists if the negative evaluation generalizes to many members of a particular ethnic group. The problem in applying this criterion to children is that highly generalized ethnic categories and labels develop relatively late in children's lives. Consequently, young children may not accurately categorize people according to their ethnicity. They may perceive certain similarities among people on the basis of one or two ethnically related attributes, but they may not be able to identify the attributes. Moreover, they tend to overdiscriminate, that is to notice more differences between people than do adults (Novak and Richman, 1980), and so generalize less. For these reasons, children may express negative evaluations toward people whom they cannot ethnically identify and with less generalization than adults. This does not necessarily mean that they are less prejudiced, but that their rudimentary attitudes have a simpler structure traceable to cognitive limitations.

The third component of a prejudiced attitude is the organized predisposition to react negatively. A predisposition to respond is simply a tendency or readiness to react in a certain way. Psychologists tend to think of predispositions much as they think of personality traits, having stability over time and consistency across situations. A predisposition, like a trait, is assumed to be present at all times in a particular person even though it is not always actively expressed. Of course, other factors present in the situation may cause the person to deviate from his or her negative predisposition. For example, fear of public disapproval or of physical retaliation may inhibit the expression of one's negative feelings at a particular time. Presumably the true predisposition shows through when the effects of other factors have been minimized. Because it is difficult to control or minimize some factors, the measurement of prejudice becomes less than perfect. In fact, because one cannot directly observe a predisposition, one can only infer its existence if the aggregation of overt negative reactions across many times and situations shows some consistency and stability. The term organized implies that the attitude is unified, that the different ways of expressing negativity hang together. The fact that young children generally show less organization and less cohesion in their behaviour alerts one to the possibility that child prejudice may also be less unified and consistent than adult prejudice. Thus, reasonable modifications must be made when applying the definition's second and third components to children's attitudes. In summary, prejudice is a unified, stable, and consistent tendency to respond in a negative way toward members of a particular ethnic group.

DEFINITIONS OF ETHNIC AWARENESS AND IDENTIFICATION

The term ethnic awareness is often used in such a general sense that it is difficult to specify exactly what people mean by it. In one sense, awareness refers to a conscious recognition of ethnicity in individuals and groups. If a North American child can point correctly to a person or photo when given the labels Black, American Indian, Chinese, White or whatever is used in that community, we say he or she possesses a form of ethnic awareness, namely ethnic/racial identification or recognition. In England, the labels used to test recognition might be White, West Indian and Asian. In France, correct recognition of a Frenchman and a Magrebian would indicate awareness. Thus, at a very simple level, being able to assign correctly the labels to the actual faces or pictures of various people indicates a basic form of perceptual ethnic awareness.

Awareness is more complex in a child who in addition notes that members of the same ethnic group possess a number of similar attributes besides their label, and that members of different ethnic groups possess different attributes. Awareness is more sophisticated when it is based not only on the perceptual process of observation, but also on the cognitive processes of generalization and categorization. One might believe that any form of ethnic awareness is bad because it leads to prejudice. Research, however, suggests that this is not so. Although initially ethnic awareness and prejudice both increase with age in young children, prejudice often declines at some later point in time while ethnic awareness remains high. That is, one can be aware of ethnicity but evaluate it and react to it either positively or negatively.

The awareness of one's own ethnicity may be even more importantly related to prejudice. Some believe that to acquire an ability to identify oneself ethnically, children need to highlight differences between themselves and others, and that the perceptual contrasts then spill over into attitude contrasts (Lambert and Klineberg, 1967). Ethnic self-identification refers to the realization that one is a member of an ethnic group, possessing attributes common to that ethnic group. Some researchers use the term ethnic identity in a broader sense to include the self as an active agent rather than solely a conceptual entity and measure it in terms of the child's adoption of feelings and behaviours that are characteristic of his or her group. This concept is not only difficult to measure but it is too inclusive to be of much value. For these reasons, I will concentrate on the narrower concept of ethnic self-identification which refers to the perceptually and cognitively based knowledge that one is a member of a particular ethnic group.

The basic component of ethnic self-identification is describing oneself in terms of a critical ethnic attribute, for example, a label or another attribute that defines rather than merely describes the ethnic group. One way to identify what are thought to be the critical attributes of an ethnic group is to ask members of that ethnic group what are the most important things about being an X (e.g. Asian, Black, French Canadian), so important that without them one could not be an X. Attributes might include ancestry or parentage, national or religious background, language, skin colour and the group's label. A second component is the recognition that one is different in certain ways from members of other ethnic groups. Knowing that one is not a member of other ethnic groups and is ethnically different from them simply clarifies that one understands the concept of ethnic group membership (this does not preclude the possibility of being a member of two groups). This component is controversial because it is assumed to be the source of prejudice. However, the reality of ethnic differences exists; denying differences can create more problems than accepting differences.

The last component is that one's ethnicity is seen to remain constant, that is, to be both consistent across changes in the context and continuous over time. If one's ethnic identification changes as a result of changes in clothing, language or age, then it is not constant. Although these criteria are more commonly found in tests of self and gender identity, they are appropriate indicators of ethnic identification as well (Rosenberg, 1979; Slaby and Frey, 1975). In fact, many of the perceptual and cognitive processes (e.g. perceptions of similarity and dissimilarity, categorization, labelling) that reflect awareness of others' ethnicity have their parallel in the above definition of self-identification.

The purpose of this first section has been to elaborate on a conceptual definition of prejudice and ethnic self-identification for the purpose of demonstrating two points. One is that the concepts have many components and are considerably more complex than most people realize. Although a conceptually complete definition would seem to be an obvious prerequisite for a credible measure, many researchers have neglected this first step. As a result, their measure lacks completeness, even though it fits our 'common sense' notion of prejudice. The second point is that an adult-oriented definition of prejudice and ethnic self-identification may not be entirely applicable to children. Certain components such as generalization, organization and constancy require cognitive capabilities that are beyond those of a child under 7 years of age. Consequently it might be useful to regard the first component of each concept as the basic definitional component, and an indication of at least an immature form of prejudice or self-identification. The other components may be absent in young children, not because they are unbiased but because they do not have the cognitive capabilities to generalize their attitude or identification.

THE MEASUREMENT OF PREJUDICE

Prejudice in children is typically assessed with one of three types of tests. The tests vary in format but all require children to evaluate members of their own and other ethnic groups. The forced-choice question format of Clark and Clark (1947) was developed in the 1930s and 1940s for use with Black American children. It has since been used in hundreds of research studies with children from many ethnic groups. Because the questions were so simple and straightforward, the answers received by Clark and Clark and by other researchers shocked people into realizing that even very young children could experience prejudice toward other groups as well as aversion toward their own. The test included seven questions in all, four of which measured attitudes. The child was shown a Black doll and a White doll (sometimes also a brown doll) and was asked to choose one doll in response to each question: Which would you like to play with? Which is the good doll? Which looks bad? Which has the nice colour?

Because the children had to choose one doll and reject the other, they could not express degrees of negativity. On a 10-point badness scale, for example, one child might rate X at 10 and Y at 1, whereas another child might rate X at 4 and Y at 3. Both children would choose X but the intensity of their negative attitude would be meaningfully different. The forced-choice data, therefore, consist only of the number of children who chose doll X in response to a particular question. The sample frequency is then statistically compared with chance levels of 50 per cent if two dolls are used and 33 per cent if three are used.

The multiple-item tests of Williams, Best and Boswell (1975) known as the Preschool Racial Attitude Measure (PRAM) and the Katz–Zalk Projective Prejudice Test (1978) overcome some of the limitations of the Doll Technique. The PRAM presents the child with 24 racial and 12 filler gender items. Each item describes a positive or negative quality. One item reads: 'Here are two girls. One of them is an ugly girl. People do not like to look at her. Which is the ugly girl?' Another item is: 'Here are two boys. One of them is a kind boy. Once he saw a kitten fall into a lake and he picked up the kitten to save it from drowning. Which is the kind boy?' The child is shown a picture of a Black and a White person and must decide which one best fits the description. The intensity of a child's positive or negative attitude is determined by summing the number of pro-White and anti-Black choices made, or the reverse. Unfortunately because each response is a forced choice, rejection of one group is confounded with acceptance of the other. When children are allowed to assign both ethnic members to the description, they do so more frequently with age (Davey, 1983; Doyle, Beaudet and Aboud, 1987). The strength of these multi-item tests is that they aggregate many evaluative adjectives in many contexts and so demonstrate generalization of the evaluation. Perhaps because of this, they have good stability over time intervals of up to one year. Incidentally, despite its name, the PRAM can be used with children up to 10 or 12 years of age.

A third type of test uses continuous rating scales which provide many rather than simply two response alternatives along a positive–negative dimension. Children are asked how much they would like a person or how close they would like to sit to a person (e.g. Aboud, 1981; Aboud and Mitchell, 1977; Genesee, Tucker and Lambert, 1978; Verna, 1981).

These measures allow the child to evaluate each ethnic member separately by locating that person on the continuum. For example, Aboud and Mitchell (1977) asked children to place photos of peers from several different ethnic groups along a 60 cm liking board, closer to themselves the more they like the peer and farther away the more they dislike the peer (see figure 1). The social distance scale developed by Verna (1981) requires children to mark on the paper how close they would want to sit to each of several own and other group members drawn on one side of the paper. The strength of this sort of measure is that each ethnic group can be evaluated independently; acceptance of one is not confounded with rejection of the other. Furthermore, several representatives of each ethnic group can be evaluated to determine whether the attitude generalizes to all members of that group. Unfortunately, only one evaluative question is typically asked, and the context does not vary as it does in the multi-item tests.

Which of these three attitude tests best fits the definition outlined earlier in the chapter? All three formats assess one's evaluation of people and so meet the first criterion. Determining whether the evaluation is elicited by the person's ethnicity and thus generalizes to many members of the group is a feature of the continuous measures and to a limited extent the multiple-item tests. Determining whether the evaluation is unified, stable and consistent is presently an excellent feature of the multiple-item tests which assess many types of evaluative responses across many situations. The forced-choice Doll Technique includes four evaluations but does not vary the situation. This feature could also be incorporated into the continuous rating scales. Thus, although each measure is somewhat limited, the combined use of a multiple-item and a continuous rating scale would assess the three criteria outlined in the definition of prejudice.

What score on these tests indicates that the child is prejudiced? Most researchers do not confront this question because they study degrees of positive and negative attitudes among groups of children. When they talk about certain children being more prejudiced than others, they simply mean that one group holds more negative attitudes. But how does one determine whether a particular child is prejudiced? Would choosing an out-group member as 'the bad one' be a sign of prejudice? Probably not. If questioned further as to how bad, the child may rate the other group as 4 out of 10 – not very bad. Furthermore, an absurd situation arises because forced-choice questions can lead to only two possible designations: prejudiced if one chooses an outgroup as the bad one, or rejecting the ingroup if one chooses one's own group as the bad one.

There are two approaches to the question of what is the cut-off point

Figure 1 Photographs of Canadian children from two age groups (8 and 9 years) used in the measurement of ethnic attitudes (White, Chinese, Black and Native Indian)

for prejudice. Williams, Best and Boswell (1975), using the 24-item PRAM scale, arbitrarily divide scores into three categories: 15 to 24 indicates prejudice against Blacks, or pro-White/anti-Black bias; 10 to 14 no prejudice; and 0 to 9 indicates prejudice against Whites or pro-Black/anti-White bias. Later Williams and Morland (1976) expanded the no-prejudice category to include scores from 8 to 16 thereby narrowing the range of prejudice scores. It is not clear how these categories were chosen other than that they divide the range of scores fairly evenly. One could likewise divide a 60 cm continuous rating scale into three ranges of scores, the top third indicating prejudice. A better strategy might be to ask children how they feel about other children whose ethnic affiliation is unknown (Rosenbaum, 1986). Their liking for these strangers would then serve as a baseline against which to compare their liking for other children whose ethnicity is known to be similar and different (Rosenbaum, 1986). For example, on a 60 cm continuous rating scale, children of similar age, sex and nationality might be rated with a mean of 40 and a range of 30 to 50. In this case, any score below 30 might indicate prejudice on the basis of ethnicity and any score above 50 would indicate a positive bias. Likewise, one could determine a baseline evaluation of the ingroup figures on the PRAM by asking children whether or not the 24 positive and negative qualities apply to the ingroup member of each item. If, for example, 8 positive items were typically assigned to the member and 8 negative items were not, the mean score of 16 would be the baseline. A range of nonbias around the score of 16 would be identified. Thus, for example, a range of scores from 14 to 18 might be used to indicate no bias, 19 to 24 to indicate pro-ingroup bias, and 0 to 13 to indicate pro-outgroup bias.

The other approach was taken by Katz, Sohn and Zalk (1975) who chose a cut-off point arbitrarily and then provided some criterial validity for that point. In other words, they found that high scorers on the Projective Prejudice Test perceived ethnic members differently than did low scorers. Although this procedure does not allow for any conclusions about children who score in the middle range, it does suggest that high scorers differ from low scorers in a number of ways all considered to reflect bias or prejudice. The two categories are therefore psychologically meaningful.

THE MEASUREMENT OF ETHNIC AWARENESS AND IDENTIFICATION

The measurement of ethnic awareness has been a haphazard affair. To provide a conceptual framework, I outlined earlier three levels of awareness of another's ethnicity: recognition or identification, perceived similarity/dissimilarity to others and cognitive categorization. The measure of recognition determines whether the child understands the meaning of the ethnic label, and can identify someone who represents that label (Clark and Clark, 1947). The request is simply: Point to the person who is an X. If there are only two alternatives to choose from, the child's selections must be significantly better than 50 per cent to demonstrate accurate recognition. If there are three alternatives, correct selections must surpass 33 per cent, and so on.

The measurement of perceived similarity and dissimilarity is somewhat more complicated because it involves the comparison of pairs of several members from more than one ethnic group. Judgements should be made along an interval scale (e.g. Aboud and Christian, 1979; Aboud and Mitchell, 1977; Genesee et al., 1978) so the child is not forced into using categories. The extent to which within-group comparisons are rated more similar than between-group comparisons indicates that the child is aware of and attentive to ethnic differences. This test is sensitive to the early stages of ethnic awareness where the child is not yet able to verbalize the use of ethnic cues but nonetheless is sporadically and inconsistently using first one and then another ethnically relevant feature to make a judgement. Katz et al. (1975) have also used this measure to assess an age-related shift from the use of ethnic cues to the use of individual features such as facial emotional expression as a basis of perceived differences. They found that with increasing age, children perceived more within-group differences, say between a sad and a happy child, and fewer differences between a Black and a White child. In light of this shift, one must recognize that there is a distinction between ethnic awareness and ethnic salience. The early increase in perceived differences between groups reflects an increase in ethnic awareness, but the later decrease is interpreted as a decline in the salience of ethnicity (though presumably awareness has not declined).

The third level of awareness, categorization, is measured by asking the child to look at a number of photographs and to put them into piles of people who belong together. The tester starts the piles by laying down photos of members of the available ethnic groups and says simply that they belong in different piles. The extent to which members are accurately assigned to their appropriate pile is the measure of ethnic awareness. Alternatively, one can request the child to go through the photographs and give each its ethnic label. This is frequently used in studies of gender awareness but rarely as a measure of ethnic awareness. Vaughan (1963) added a difficult twist to the categorization task by including members of one ethnic group dressed in the clothes of the other. To categorize the people accurately, one needed to focus on facial features and ignore the misleading attire. The task therefore measured whether the child was using the correct ethnic cue rather than the incorrect clothing cue to categorize, and is thus similar to the measure of constancy in self-identification. Once again a distinction can be made between responses that reflect awareness and those that reflect salience. Davey (1983) assessed the salience of ethnicity by simply asking the child to put the photos into piles of people who belong together. The photos varied along four dimensions, including, for example, race and gender, and so the attribute used for the first sorting was considered most salient for that child. Then the photos from only one pile were returned to the child and he/she was told to put those into piles of people who belong together. The attribute used for the second sorting was considered of secondary salience, and so on. Multidimensional scaling is another more complicated way of determining the basis of categorization (Aboud and Christian, 1979; Jones and Ashmore, 1973).

The measure of ethnic self-identification uses many of these same procedures with the self as the target stimulus. Again, for very young children it is awareness or knowledge of one's ethnicity that the researcher wants to assess. Once awareness is established, the question becomes how salient is ethnicity in comparison to other attributes as a way of identifying oneself. The perceived relation between self and others involves paired comparisons of the self and more than one member from more than one ethnic group (Aboud and Christian, 1979; Genesee et al., 1978). For example, Aboud and Mitchell (1977) used a 60 cm similarity board positioned from left to right in front of the child. Two representatives, one a stick figure labelled with the child's name and one a photographed ethnic member, were given to the child who placed them on the board, closer the more similar they were and farther apart the more different. The distance between was taken as an index of dissimilarity. Accurate self-identification is indexed by greater perceived similarity (or less dissimilarity) to ingroup members than to other group members. Few researchers have used a self-categorization measure but one could presumably include a photo of the child to be sorted along with the other photos. Likewise, one could assess the child's awareness of his/her own label by providing a selection of labels and asking the child, 'What are you?' (Aboud, 1980). One would want to check by asking about each rejected label, 'Are you an X?' Finally, awareness of one's ethnic constancy is assessed using one of the procedures developed by Slaby and Frey (1975) or Marcus and Overton (1978). The continuity questions might take the following form: 'What ethnicity were you when you were born?' and 'What will you be ten years from now?' The consistency questions describe a superficial transformation such as in clothing or in appearance and then ask for an ethnic identification (Aboud, 1984; Aboud and Skerry, 1983). For example, Aboud (1984) showed White children a series of five photographs depicting a White Canadian boy as he put on Native Indian clothing. In the final photo, the boy's appearance except for his face had changed as a result of the clothing transformation (see figure 2). Constancy is assessed by asking the child to ethnically identify the boy in the last photo. If the child answers that the boy is White, he/she is also asked if the boy is Indian (i.e. the rejected label) to make sure only one label is applied. Semaj (1980) asked the question hypothetically of Black children: If a Black child wore a blond wig, would he/she be a Black or a White child? Constancy is indexed by the consistent identification of one's ethnic group despite the passage of time or the change in appearance.

The most frequently used question to assess self-identification is the one used originally in Clark and Clark's (1947) Doll Technique. They asked, 'Which one looks like you?' The child is required to make a forced choice, that is to make an all-or-none judgement about his/her appearance. In this sense, it is like a categorizing judgement and

Figure 2   Three of the five photographs showing a clothing transformation and used in the measurement of ethnic constancy

probably says something about the child's ability to categorize on the basis of appearance. However, because the association is made with only one member of an ethnic group, the identification may not be reliable. Researchers should present several examples from each ethnic group in order to compare the number of own group versus other group members identified with.

SUMMARY

The purpose of this first chapter has been to examine what the concept of prejudice means to psychology researchers. Although the most critical component is a negative evaluation, other components include a generalization to many members of a particular ethnic group, and the presence of a unified, stable and consistent tendency to react negatively. Unfortunately, certain measures of prejudice do not incorporate these different components and so do not adequately assess prejudice. However, it was also pointed out that certain components may be absent in children under 7 years, not because they are unbiased but because they are cognitively less able to generalize. Another problem is determining what degree of negative evaluation and what score on the test constitutes prejudice. Several strategies for identifying prejudice were offered.

Similarly, the concepts of ethnic awareness and ethnic self-identification were discussed. Again, a number of components were identified and the relevant measures described. Because these two concepts are concerned mostly with perceptual and cognitive processes, it is clearer than in the case of prejudice that not all components will be present in young children.

2 Theories of Prejudice

Why might a child be prejudiced? Why does a child say that an ethnically different child is bad and reject him as a playmate? Let us assume that the child expresses such negative attitudes consistently, so that we are dealing with a relatively enduring prejudice, not just a momentary flash of anger. Is it because the child was born with a predisposition to be aggressive and hateful toward those who are different? Or is it because the child was taught to be prejudiced toward certain groups? If a representative sample of adults were asked these questions, there would probably be some who support the idea of a predisposition and some who insist that prejudice is entirely learned. Those who support the inborn predisposition theory might point to evidence that very broadminded parents often have very prejudiced youngsters. Those who support a learning theory would claim that 2-year-olds are generally not prejudiced but that 12-year-olds could very well be, so prejudice must have been learned in the intervening years. Furthermore, they point to the well-known fact that some parents express prejudiced ideas to their children, such as telling them not to play with certain children because they are bad.

Most people hold to a particular theory of prejudice and are able to support it with evidence from their own experience. Scientific theories of prejudice do not differ substantially from our everyday theories. However, for a scientific theory to be a 'good' explanation of prejudice, it must also adequately address certain facts that researchers know to be true about prejudice. For example, certain groups are the target of more intense prejudice than others. Also, certain individuals in a given society and certain societies are more prejudiced than others. Finally, a good theory must account for the development of prejudice and for the differences between child and adult forms of prejudice. In the final analysis, a theory is validated not by a handful of anecdotal experiences but by many studies that systematically test its propositions.

Two types of explanations have emerged from theories of prejudice. One is that our attitudes and thoughts about ethnic groups simply reflect the structure of society. Groups possessing different power and status will be viewed and valued differently (see Morland and Suthers, 1980). If they are in competition, then ingroup and outgroup will be viewed and valued differently (Sherif and Sherif, 1969; Tajfel, 1978). These theories will be discussed under the heading social reflection theory. The second explanation is that prejudice reflects an internal state, a cluster of motivations, cognitions or emotions that predisposes the person to dislike different others (Adorno et al., 1950). This will be referred to as an inner state theory of prejudice.

SOCIAL REFLECTION THEORY OF PREJUDICE

This theory claims that prejudice simply reflects the differential values attached to different groups in a stratified society. People are essentially a product of their social milieu; they adopt attitudes and stereotypes about groups that correspond to the relative power and status held by those groups. Presumably they form attitudes only after they have acquired this social knowledge about power and status from other people or the media. That is, awareness of the social structure must precede the formation of attitudes and stereotypes. The implication is that by 12 years of age, when children know the structure of their society, all children should show prejudice that reflects the status differences of groups. This is indeed not the case.

A more palatable version of this theory is that children adopt attitudes corresponding to the social structure as perceived by their parents and significant others. The personal value system of parents may differ from the value system based on relative power or status. For example, personal values are often determined by affiliation; people like their ingroup and dislike outgroups. Children then learn to evaluate groups the way their parents do either by direct training or by observing and imitating their parents' verbal and nonverbal behaviour. According to Allport (1954), direct training of prejudice is rare. More frequently children imitate their parents' attitude because they identify with their parents or want to please them. Very young children may imitate the label and its associated emotion without knowing the group referred to by the label. According to Allport, when children understand what group is referred to by the label, their negative emotion becomes crystallized into a negative attitude and total rejection of the group. Later it becomes integrated with their whole personality and thus becomes stabilized and hard to change.

This version of the theory suggests a particular course of development of prejudice. Young children are presumably unprejudiced. Allport (1954, p. 289) believes that 'four-year-olds are normally interested, curious, and appreciative of differences in racial groups'. It is not clear from this theory at what age children will learn to imitate the labels and emotions of their parents, but it is presumably a gradual process, aided by the child's identification with his/her parents and by the desire to please them. Once the label generalizes to all members of the group, that is once the child is able to categorize, prejudice becomes generalized and stable. One would expect to see an increase in prejudice at this point and again when the prejudice becomes integrated with the child's personality.

Empirical research, to be discussed in chapter 3, does not support these developmental predictions. Four-year-olds hold strong prejudices toward different racial and ethnic groups, and prejudice does not continue to become exaggerated with age. There are other weak points to the theory. It assumes that young children have a mental vacuum, and that they absorb everything their parents tell them. If they identify with and want to please a parent, they adopt his or her attitudes. This view of the young child as an indiscriminate vacuum suction is not supported by empirical research. It also cannot explain why children from minority ethnic groups do not adopt their parents' attitudes. These children often prefer an outgroup over their own group. Likewise, young children from 'gender liberated' homes often hold conventional attitudes about male and female sex roles despite their parents' egalitarian attitudes. Children are not mere templates of their parents, or of the media for that matter. The social reflection explanation is therefore generally limited in its developmental aspects; not only is it unable to account for many of the age-related changes in prejudice but it treats the determinants of prejudice the same regardless of age. Another major weakness is the lack of explanation for individual differences, the fact that some people in a given society are more prejudiced than others.

Despite these weaknesses, the social reflection theory has some strong points. For example, it explains why certain ethnic groups are derogated more than others. In other words, it explains the selection of certain targets for prejudice. Groups that are lowest in status and power in a society are expected to be most derogated, if attitudes reflect the structure of society. Alternatively, if groups are perceived as somewhat equal and in competition, the competing group will be most derogated. Thus, the theory provides a testable explanation as to why all groups other than one's own are not disliked equally. The theory is also able to explain why prejudice is so widespread and why it has persisted across generations. Presumably all societies that are stratified or competitive will evidence prejudice. It persists because parents who have learned their prejudices from their own parents now pass them on to their children.

INNER STATE THEORY OF PREJUDICE

The theory of Adorno et al. (1950) explains prejudice in terms of an internal conflict that has not been resolved. The internal conflict is between the desire to be good and the fact that in reality one is not always good. According to the psychodynamic view of childhood on which this theory is based, all children experience hostility toward their parents when they are prevented from doing what they want to do. Frustration and disagreement inevitably lead to aggression and anger. Most parents disapprove of and punish aggression especially if it is directed at themselves. Children learn, then, that their aggression and hostility are bad; they feel anxious and guilty. According to psychodynamic theory, this sequence of frustration, hostility, punishment and anxiety is the natural course of events, and is therefore not in itself the cause of prejudice.

Prejudice results from child-rearing practices that interfere with the healthy resolution of this conflict. Descriptions of these practices and of parents were gleaned from interviews with prejudiced and unprejudiced adults. Unprejudiced people tended to have parents who accepted their individual qualities and who helped them express their aggression openly in modified and controlled ways. Such people learned to express their hostility to parents or other authority figures in an appropriate way. In contrast, prejudiced people tended to have parents who, to enhance or maintain their own social status, imposed rigid conventional rules of conduct on their children. The rules, for example, prohibited aggression and hostility toward one's parents, the reason being that higher status people should be treated with respect, and that anti-social impulses must be rooted out if one is to gain status in society. All anti-social impulses such as hostility were severely punished. The theory claims that because of their parents' punitiveness, prejudiced people never learn to express hostility to their parents or to authority figures. Instead they displace this hostility on to people who lack authority and power, that is on to minority groups. Prejudiced people are also not able to accept such hostility as part of their experience. Instead, they deny feeling anti-social impulses and project these negative impulses onto others. Prejudice therefore stems from an inability to accept and control one's aggressive impulses as a result of the harsh way in which one's parents dealt with them.

One strength of this theory is that it accounts for individual differences in the levels of prejudice. It can explain why some people are intensely prejudiced and others very tolerant. The theory explains individual differences in terms of different styles of child-rearing that lead to differences in impulse control. Another strength of the theory is that it explains the stability of prejudice, that is, why adults maintain their prejudices even when they move to a different society. According to the theory, prejudiced people may find a different minority group to derogate, may find a different target for their prejudice, but the level of prejudice remains because it is tied to a stable inner state. This is explained in terms of the important role played by parents and by developments in the early years which determine the child's enduring personality traits, one of which is prejudice. Prejudice is viewed as one aspect of the person's personality structure, and being part of an organized structure, it does not readily change on its own. The theory also explains very well the intensity with which some people maintain their prejudice, despite peer disapproval. Their attitudes seem to be based on something more ego-involving than simply imitation or conformity. They appear to be energized by a strongly personal force involving conflict and intense emotions.

One weakness of the theory is in not specifying what targets are selected for prejudice. The social reflection theory is able to explain why certain outgroups are singled out for derogation. The inner state theory claims that all minority groups, ethnic and otherwise, are treated similarly by prejudiced persons. The only specification of target groups is that they be weak, unfamiliar and different from parents, namely low status and powerless groups. Powerless groups are convenient targets of prejudice because unlike authority figures they cannot retaliate. This minimizes the prejudiced person's anxiety. Moreover, the less that is known about the group, the easier it is to assign negative traits to it. In these two ways, minority ethnic members are convenient targets for both displaced anger and projected traits.

Although this theory provides a great deal of detail about the childhood antecedents of prejudice, it makes no distinction between the prejudices of a child and those of an adult. It makes no prediction about age changes in prejudice emphasizing instead the stability of prejudice. One might extend the theory by suggesting that regardless of parental assistance, most children are unable to control their hostility or to integrate good and bad qualities in themselves because of their emotional and cognitive limitations. Consequently, one might predict that all young children would be prejudiced and that prejudice would decline with development. This prediction is compatible with the theory but not part of it.

A SOCIAL–COGNITIVE DEVELOPMENTAL THEORY OF PREJUDICE

Dissatisfaction with the developmental aspects of these two classical theories led to the emergence of social-cognitive developmental theories of prejudice (Katz, 1976; Piaget and Weil, 1951). These theories predict qualitatively different types of prejudice at different ages as a result of changes in cognitive structure. My own view is that these structural changes predict non-gradual changes in the level of prejudice with age. Thus, prejudice may be regarded as inevitable but not necessarily enduring because it is based on inevitable aspects of a young child's way of thinking which eventually disappear. Even though cognitive limitations determine the structure of attitudes, daily input from the environment presumably affects the content, i.e. about which ethnic groups one has an attitude. However, even at the level of content, the theory would claim that the child's cognitive limitations filter and distort environmental input. Consequently, the child does not accurately take in or understand everything he/she hears or sees. A critical change in prejudice takes place around 7 years of age as children move from preoperational to concrete operational ways of thinking (Piaget, 1932). Children younger than 7 years are handicapped by many cognitive limitations which interfere with a full understanding of the basis of ethnicity and the individuals who make up ethnic groups. The prejudice seen in 4- to 7-year-olds is therefore qualitatively different from the prejudice seen in 7- to 12-year-olds.

Piaget's cognitive developmental explanation of prejudice assumes that preferences develop parallel to cognitive processes. Preferences can therefore be described in terms of a three-stage sequence of cognitive development, based on the changing faces of egocentrism (Piaget and Weil, 1951). Egocentrism refers to the self-centred understanding children have of their world; they assume that other people experience the world as they do because that is the correct and only way. From 4 to 7 years of age, children are egocentric and unaware of national or ethnic groups. Piaget considered the preferences of this stage to be whimsical; that is, they are based on random personal considerations. From 7 to 10 years, children decentre from themselves but become sociocentric, meaning that they focus on their own group rather than solely on themselves. This focus, however, prevents them from understanding other groups. Other groups are recognized only in ways that contrast and thereby highlight the features of the children's own group. Preferences change to fit these contrasting group perceptions in that children become positive toward their own group and negative toward other groups. From 10 to 15 years of age, children undergo more extensive decentration and integration, allowing them to distinguish among other groups and to apply the principle of reciprocity to these groups. This last stage is not clearly described and it is difficult to say whether prejudice would remain high or be reduced at this age. Reciprocity refers to symmetry in a relationship. It implies that one can accept the validity of different perspectives; for example, one can grant to another person the ingroup preferences that one holds toward one's own group. If one remains focused on groups, this would lead to the notion of group reciprocity, that is each group holds its own prejudice and suspicion of the other. Thus, reciprocity between groups might serve to justify reciprocal hate.

There are at least two apparent limitations to Piaget's theory. One is that decentration does not stop at an awareness of group differences but continues to the point where children focus on individuals within these groups. Piaget did not consider the implications of such a shift to individuals and to individual rather than group reciprocity. Reciprocity with respect to individuals might take the form: 'I am a good person according to my group and he is a good person according to his group; therefore he may have some good qualities just as I do.' A second limitation is the vague explanation of early preferences. Processes that determine preferences during the egocentric stage are not specified because it is assumed that they are random and different for each child. However, the evidence does not support this assumption. The ethnic preferences of egocentric children are similar to one another and appear to be systematic. A systematic explanation must be offered.

My own version of social-cognitive developmental theory explains the development of ethnic attitudes in terms of two overlapping sequences of development. One sequence involves the process that dominates a child's experience: from affective states to perceptions and finally to cognitions. The second sequence involves the focus of one's attention: from self to groups and finally to individuals. The major implication of a sequence of steps is that at any particular age the child's way of relating to ethnic groups will be determined by his/her present level, that is by the process and focus of attention that dominate at that time. Furthermore, the child will be most influenced by information that fits his/her present level.

According to the first sequence, children are initially dominated by their emotions and preferences, that is by the affective process. Their prejudice will therefore be determined by their emotions and by need satisfactions, and not by their ethnic self-identification. Information about a person that is relevant to affective processes rather than to group membership will be most influential. For example, wariness and fear are aroused by strangers who look different. Children begin to be wary of strangers at 9 to 12 months of age. By 3 years of age, their wariness may be less pervasive but may extend to strangers who are different and unpredictable. In addition, children are happiest when their wants are met, and so they feel happiest about another person who has good things to satisfy his/her needs. According to research on preferences, they prefer a child who receives goodies over one who gives out goodies or one who receives none (Gottfried and Gottfried, 1974). Thus, attitudes in this first stage are determined by fear and happiness.

At the second step of this sequence, perceptions of others develop relative to oneself. Children notice how similar or dissimilar other people are to themselves. Prejudice will therefore be determined by perceptions of dissimilarity. Dissimilar people are disliked. Children at this level rely on perceptions rather than cognitions in the sense that they are dominated by what they can see, by external observables rather than by internal qualities. People who are dissimilar in skin colour, language, clothing and hair texture are most saliently noticed as different. These perceptions form the basis of ethnic self-identification. Children identify themselves by noting to whom they are similar. When perceptions begin to dominate their experience, children may modify their preferences to bring them into line with self-perceptions, where previously self-perceptions may have been distorted to fit preferences.

At the third step of this sequence, cognitive understanding develops. Children begin to understand categories and individual qualities of people. They begin to understand the basis of ethnicity, namely, that one's ethnicity is not based on desire or on the clothing one wears but on more permanent and objective criteria such as ancestry. Also, the ability to decentre, or to attend simultaneously to two or more different perspectives, allows the child to accept different but reciprocal preferences and perceptions in another person.

Cognitive development should herald a neutralization of the bipolar and intense preferences of the young child. The awareness of an individual's internal qualities, the understanding that ethnicity is largely unchangeable, and that ethnic differences are reconcilable, all serve to reduce prejudice in the 8- to 10-year-old child. At this step, children should be most responsive to information and interventions which appeal to these cognitive processes.

The second sequence of development overlapping with the affect–

perception–cognition sequence involves a change in the child's focus of attention. Very young children are most aware of themselves, and of their own preferences and perceptions. Later, children emphasize categories of people, and view people as members of these categories or groups. Still later, children revert to an emphasis on individuals, but this time the self and others are viewed in terms of their own unique qualities.

In the first step of this sequence, the egocentric child's emphasis on self has been well documented in many different domains. Children under 7 years of age are basically single-minded. They assume that other people see objects the way they do even when their orientations to the object must necessarily produce different images (e.g. one sees the front of a person and the other sees the back). Similarly, young children assume that other people know what they do and experience the same emotions that they do in a given situation. Any different feeling is necessarily wrong.

The second step is much like Piaget's sociocentric stage. Prejudice follows from a preoccupation with groups and specifically the differences between one's own and other groups. Children initially exaggerate the contrasts in order to clarify their understanding of the groups, and this may serve to exaggerate their attitudes into a pro–anti dichotomy. Later, though still preoccupied with people as members of groups, they become aware of the similarities as well as the differences between their own and other groups. This change reflects some cognitive flexibility. Thus, the initial decline in prejudice may be seen in children who are still focusing on groups but have greater cognitive flexibility.

The third step of this sequence which involves greater attention to individuals should be accompanied by even lower levels of prejudice. Because people are judged in terms of their unique personalities, they will be liked or disliked for personal rather than ethnic group qualities. This is not to say that all people will be evaluated positively, but the criterion will not be ethnic group membership. This step does not eliminate the use of or need for ethnic stereotypes when personal information is unavailable or too extensive to process efficiently (Rothbart, Fulero, Jensen, Howard and Birrell, 1978).

The three-step shift from self to group to individual has also been incorporated in two related areas of social development, namely Kohlberg's (1976) theory of moral development and Block's (1973) theory of sex-role development. Moral judgement is initially tied to what the child would or would not enjoy (called naive hedonism); then it is tied to social rules laid down by authority (called conventional); and finally it is based on personally evaluated principles. Similarly, Block

(1973) suggests that the way one views one's own sex-role and prescribes sex-appropriate behaviour changes with age. Initially, children define sex-appropriate behaviour in terms of what they want to do. During the conformist or conventional stage, children rely on social stereotypes about males and females to determine what is appropriate. In other words, people are viewed as members of a gender group, and gender stereotypes are viewed as rules that prescribe how such members should act. Some time later, children begin to differentiate within these two gender categories until they finally realize that an individual can be more flexible than stereotypes allow, and that personal inclination rather than social rules should dictate the way one is.

Block's theory is in fact a theory of sex-role identity, in which the child grows into and then out of a group-based definition of him/herself. Block describes a mature identity as secure enough in one's own identity to be able to adopt attributes that are considered socially to be more appropriate for the opposite sex (or we could substitute, for the other ethnic group). A male who can describe himself in terms of female stereotype attributes as well as male stereotype attributes, and a female who can do likewise are considered to have mature gender identities. With some elaboration, Block's theory can make some interesting points about ethnic identity and attitudes. If children define and evaluate themselves in group terms, they are likely to do the same for others. If they base their identification on individual rather than group attributes, then they are likely to identify and evaluate others in terms of their individual attributes. Furthermore, one of the attributes considered to be characteristic of another group is to like their own group. Thus, someone with a mature ethnic identity could like members of that other group without feeling conflict or insecurity.

SUMMARY OF THEORIES OF PREJUDICE

The most popular theory of prejudice and the one most widely accepted by the general public and the research community is the social reflection theory. In fact, there are at least two theories which claim that children's prejudice reflects existing social values. One theory claims that prejudice reflects the differential values given to different ethnic groups in a stratified society. Because these differential values are based on the status of the groups, the same set of values will be known by all members of the society. Thus, the positive and negative values attached to different ethnic groups will be the same for all children regardless of their own ethnic membership. The second social reflection theory states that children's attitudes reflect their parents' values, namely a preference for one's own group and a rejection of outgroups. In short, attitudes are tied to one's ethnic group membership. Both social reflection theories assume that gradual learning is the process by which children acquire social values and attitudes. Thus, prejudice should increase gradually with age.

The authoritarian theory of prejudice explains negative attitudes in terms of states internal to the child rather than social ones. Conflict between what the child wants and what is available leads to anger. Unless parents help the child express this anger in modified and controlled ways, it will be displaced on to outsiders who are less powerful and less known than one's parents. Unless the child is able to integrate both the good and the bad in him or herself, the bad parts will be projected on to unknown and powerless people. This theory emphasizes that anger and the use of defence mechanisms to deal with the anger are the sources of prejudice, but that parents who use authoritarian child-rearing practices are also responsible.

Social-cognitive developmental theories claim that prejudice is inevitable in young children because of their cognitive limitations. The prejudice seen in a child at one developmental stage is qualitatively different from the prejudice of a child at another stage because it arises out of a different understanding of the social world. Piaget considered prejudice to be an outcome of first egocentric and then sociocentric perceptions of the social world. My own view is that the intensity, the direction and the social forces influencing prejudice are determined by two overlapping sequences of development: one is the shift from affective to perceptual to cognitive processes, and the other is a change in focus from self to groups to individuals. These changes coincide to a certain extent with the shift from preoperational to concrete operational forms of thinking and also with other social-cognitive changes taking place within the latter stage.

Each theory has its strengths and its weaknesses in terms of how it accounts for individual, cultural, target and developmental differences in prejudice. In addition the theories will later be evaluated in terms of whether they are consistent with the age trends reported in the empirical literature and in terms of the evidence supporting the influence of relevant social and psychological factors.

3   The Development of Ethnic Attitudes and Prejudice

The purpose of the previously discussed theories is to explain why people are prejudiced. In each case, there was a clear statement about how prejudice develops in the child. From this, we inferred the age at which it was expected to appear and how it would change with age. One way to test the theories, then, is to examine empirically at what age prejudice first appears, and whether it increases (social reflection prediction), decreases (social-cognitive development prediction), or remains stable with age (authoritarian prediction). In this chapter, a comprehensive review will be made of the empirical research related to this issue.

The research findings will be organized to address the following theoretically interesting questions.

1 At what age are ethnic attitudes first acquired?
2 How do attitudes change thereafter during the preadolescent years?
3 Is prejudice toward other groups related to favouritism toward one's own group?
4 Do attitudes toward own and other groups differ for majority and minority children?

Thus, the key organizing variables will initially be the child's age, the child's ethnic background, and own versus other group targets. Whether these variables are causally relevant to prejudice, and more generally, what variables determine the development of prejudice will be discussed later. To answer the question of why children hold negative ethnic attitudes, we will evaluate factors such as self-esteem, parental values, exposure to other ethnic groups and cognitive development. Before tackling that question, we must specify which children are prejudiced and at what ages.

An examination of research reported in the literature over the past 20 years revealed that ethnic attitudes are acquired around 3 or 4 years of age, and usually change during the following 8 years. Whether the favouritism is directed toward one's own or another group depends quite strongly on the child's majority/minority status. Because most but not all of the studies were conducted in ethnically heterogeneous and stratified societies such as the United States, Canada and Great Britain, our conclusions must be limited to these particular conditions and the effects they have on status. The conditions in these and many other countries place certain groups in a minority role with lower social, political and economic status than other groups. Although in themselves these conditions may not be sufficient, it is clear that they set the stage for prejudice to develop. In other words, certain societies promote prejudice more that others because of the relations that have been established between the groups. This means that prejudice is not a universal phenomenon and that it is safe to generalize the conclusions drawn here only to similarly structured societies.

Prejudice has most often been noted among majority group children, so we will begin the discussion with the development of their attitudes. Following this, the attitudes of minority children will be reviewed.

WHITE MAJORITY CHILDREN'S ATTITUDES TO OTHER GROUPS

White children as young as 3 years of age have expressed negative attitudes toward Blacks. However, prejudice becomes considerably more prevalent, and well documented, among 4-year-olds (Asher and Allen, 1969; Kircher and Furby, 1971; Renninger and Williams, 1966; Vaughan, 1964). This is disputed by Brown and Johnson (1971) who found that children younger than 5 years of age did not assign more negative attributes to Blacks than to Whites. In any case, there is strong evidence that most White children between the ages of 3 and 5 choose a Black person as looking 'bad', as having negative qualities or as being least preferred as a playmate (Asher and Allen, 1969; Clark, Hocevar and Dembo, 1980; Crooks, 1970; Greenwald and Oppenheim, 1968; Morland, 1966; Renninger and Williams, 1966; Rohrer, 1977; Vaughan, 1964). When the sample includes children from 5 to 7 years, the results are quite clear, with two-thirds and generally more claiming that the Asian, Black or Native Indian is bad or disliked (Aboud, 1977, 1980; Asher and Allen, 1969; Brown and Johnson, 1971; Clark, Hocevar and Dembo, 1980; Corenblum and Wilson, 1982; Fox and Jordan, 1973; Friedman, 1980; Goldstein, Koopman and Goldstein, 1979; Gregor and McPherson, 1966a; Gregor and McPherson, 1966b; Hraba and Grant, 1970; Hunsberger, 1976; Klein, Levine and Charry, 1979; Madge, 1976; Marsh, 1970; Milner, 1973; Morland and Hwang, 1981; Vaughan, 1964;

Williams, Best and Boswell, 1975). Some of these studies statistically compared the responses of children at different age levels and found that prejudice increased between the ages of 4 and 7 years (Asher and Allen, 1969; Brown and Johnson, 1971; Clark et al., 1980; Hraba and Grant, 1970; Vaughan, 1964; Williams et al., 1975).

After the age of 7, a very interesting phenomenon occurs. Many studies reported that prejudice began to decline around the age of 7 or 8 years. Children were less likely to consider an Asian, Black or Native Indian as looking 'bad', as having negative qualities or as being least preferred as a playmate. They still expressed a bias, but the bias was less strong after the age of 7 or 8 than it had been before (Aboud, 1980; Aboud and Mitchell, 1977; Asher and Allen, 1969; Brown and Johnson, 1971; Clark et al., 1980; Friedman, 1980; George and Hoppe, 1979; Kalin, 1979; Katz and Zalk, 1978; Vaughan, 1964; Williams et al., 1975; Zinser, Rich and Bailey, 1981).

This decline in prejudice is interesting because it is contrary to what is expected from a social reflection theory of prejudice (i.e. that prejudice will increase with age and social learning), and it is contrary to what was reported by Brand, Ruiz and Padilla (1974) in their earlier review of the prejudice research. They concluded from their review that prejudice increased with age in White children. I found no studies reported in the past 20 years that support this conclusion. To be fair, there are still some studies that do not find a decline in prejudice; they find that prejudice remains at the same level from 7 to 12 years (Asher and Allen, 1969; Davey, 1983; Epstein, Krupat and Obudho, 1976; Genesee, Tucker and Lambert, 1978; Katz, Sohn and Zalk, 1975). Other studies have assessed high levels of prejudice but have not analysed for age differences (Hunsberger, 1978; Stephan and Rosenfield, 1979; Tajfel, Jahoda, Nemeth, Rim and Johnson, 1972; Tajfel, Nemeth, Jahoda, Campbell and Johnson, 1970; Verna, 1982; Williams and Morland, 1976). In any case, more than half of the studies of White children between the ages of 7 and 12 show a decline in negative attitudes toward other groups.

The decline in prejudice is somewhat controversial, attributed by some to a superficial response bias and by others to a profound change in attitudes. This issue will be dealt with more thoroughly in chapters 5 and 6 when testing procedures and causal determinants of prejudice are discussed. The controversy is relevant to testing procedures because those who explain the decline in prejudice as a superficial response alteration feel that the fault lies with the tests used. Katz et al. (1975) claim that projective tests of prejudice, which hide the intent of the questions, are less subject to response alteration. This may be true, although the issue being discussed, namely the decline in prejudice after age 7, has been observed with projective (e.g. Brown and Johnson, 1971) as well as with nonprojective tests (e.g. Asher and Allen, 1969; George and Hoppe, 1979).

Here, in more detail, are some of the procedures and results found with White children. Several studies reporting a decline in prejudice with age will first be described. Asher and Allen (1969) used the original Doll Technique developed by Clark and Clark (1947). They showed children from 3 to 8 years of age a Black puppet with medium brown skin colour and black hair and a White puppet with light skin and light hair. In other respects, the two puppets were identical. The children were asked a series of questions by an examiner of their own race: 'Which puppet is the nice puppet? Which puppet would you like to play with? Which puppet looks bad? Which puppet is the nice colour?' The number of children pointing to the Black puppet was compared with the number pointing to the White puppet. The number of children nominating a Black puppet was significantly lower on the positive items (20 per cent, 22 per cent, 20 per cent, respectively) and higher on the negative item (77 per cent) than the number nominating a White puppet. Responses to only one of the four items changed with age: the Black puppet was chosen as having the nice colour by 33 per cent of 3- and 4-year-olds, down to 16 per cent of 5- and 6-year-olds, and up to 41 per cent of 7- and 8-year-olds. These results indicate that prejudice was present in children as young as 3 and 4 years of age, and that it was maintained at the same high level on three out of four items. One item indicated an increase and then decrease in prejudice with age. Using a similar forced-choice procedure with photos instead of puppets, Vaughan (1964) asked, 'Which child would you choose for a playmate?' The percentage of White children choosing a Maori (a Brown Polynesian New Zealander) changed from 25 per cent at 4 years to 0 per cent at 6 and 8 years, 30 per cent at 10 years and 40 per cent at 12 years. The increasing avoidance of Maoris from 4 to 8 years and the subsequent decline in prejudice from 8 to 12 years is quite evident in these data. Similarly, George and Hoppe (1979) asked children from 7 to 12 years which person they would not like as a friend. They had four photos to choose from: a White, an Asian, a Black and a Native Indian. The children were more likely to reject a Black than an Asian or Indian, and this declined with age from 64 per cent at 8 years to 34 per cent at 10 years and finally to 19 per cent at 12 years. These percentages should be compared with a chance level of 25 per cent which would be the expected proportion if rejections were randomly distributed across the four ethnic photos. Only the 8-year-olds showed significant bias against Blacks; the older children did not show such bias.

Such studies have not gone uncriticized. One weakness is that the conclusions are based on responses to only a few items, as many as four items in the Asher and Allen (1969) study and as few as one item in the other two studies. Are these responses reliable? In other words, would the children give the same prejudiced answer if asked ten or twenty questions instead of only one? Findings based on the multiple-item PRAM indicate that they do. This measure presents children with 24 positive and negative evaluative descriptions. The children are asked to point to the Black or the White person whom they think fits the description. Choosing the White person for the positive items and the Black person for the negative items on at least 17 of the 24 items indicates definite bias, according to the authors (Williams and Morland, 1976). The results indicate that children from 3 to 5 years of age had an average biased score of 17.0, that this increased to 18.3 and 19.0 at 6 and 7 years of age, and then decreased to 16.4 and 15.6 at 8 and 9 years, respectively. It seems then that even when many items are used to measure prejudice, White children show a definite bias against Blacks in the preschool years and at 6 and 7 years. In summarizing the results of many such studies, Williams and Morland (1976) state that 72 per cent of children in this age group showed a definite bias. They also obtained a much lower level of prejudice from children older than 7 years whose scores were in the unbiased range.

A second major criticism of these studies is that prejudice toward the other group is confounded with preference for one's own. Because the children are allowed to choose only one person, their preference for their own group necessarily results in a rejection of the other. There is no way to express preference for one's own group and liking for the other. Morland has attempted to overcome this measurement problem by asking, 'Would you like to play with these children?' A yes answer registers acceptance, a no answer with a racial justification indicates rejection, and a no answer with a nonracial justification indicates nonacceptance. The results of twelve or so studies reveal that White children overwhelmingly accept to play with Black children (Williams and Morland, 1976). The measure does not seem to show any variance; it does not discriminate between children. The problem may be a response bias; when in doubt, people prefer to say yes than to say no (as most referendum organizers well know). Furthermore, because the justifications for affirmative answers are not coded, we do not know whether the choice is based on a positive quality of the person or on the desire to play with anyone simply for the sake of playing.

Other attempts to overcome the problem of confounding own and other group attitudes include the use of separate and independent ratings of each group. In the Aboud and Mitchell (1977) study, we showed 6- and 8-year-old children photographs of boys from their own and three other ethnic groups: Asian, Hispanic and Native Indian. There were two boys from each group. Before expressing their attitudes, the children were asked to identify the ethnicity of each boy by pointing to the ones who fit each of the four ethnic labels. The children were for the most part very accurate; whenever they were not, they were corrected and the procedure repeated. This identification was necessary to ensure that the children perceived the persons as intended, that is as members of the four ethnic groups. Then their attitudes were assessed using the 60 cm liking board. They placed a photo closer to themselves at the zero cm end the more they liked him, and farther away the more they disliked him. The average distance from self of the two representatives of each group was analysed (see figure 3). The group factor was not defined in terms of ethnicity but in terms of four subjectively defined categories: own group, most-liked other group, middle-liked other group, and disliked other group. By using each child's own evaluative categories rather than objective ethnicity, we could isolate two important attitudes: the children's most positive attitude toward an outgroup and their most

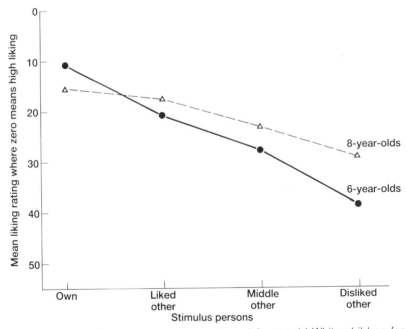

Figure 3   Mean liking ratings made by 6- and 8-year-old White children for own and 3 other ethnic groups (data from Aboud and Mitchell, 1977)

negative attitude towards an outgroup. Specifically, we could address the questions: Do children prefer their own group over all others or over just some others, and do children evaluatively distinguish among other ethnic groups?

The children from both age groups liked their own ethnic group. However, there were interesting differences between the 6- and the 8-year-olds. The younger children liked their own more than the other three groups, but nonetheless distinguished among the latter three. There was indeed one group that each child did not like though there was little agreement on which group it was. The older children liked Whites slightly less than the younger children and liked another group as much as their own. They were also less negative, actually quite neutral, toward their disliked group. In general then, the older children held less exaggerated attitudes and dichotomized less between own and other groups.

There are several limitations to this study. One is that the results are based on only one attitudinal item, namely liking. No other evaluative dimension is considered. Most people would consider liking to be a critical aspect of an attitude but multiple items enhance the reliability and validity of a measure. However, there are a few strong points worth mentioning in comparison with other results. One is that attitudes toward other groups became less negative with age even though ingroup attitudes changed only slightly. Thus, the reduction in prejudice toward others found in forced-choice studies is not solely a reflection of disenchantment with one's own group. A second strong point is that White children do not appear as uniformly prejudiced toward all other groups when they have the opportunity to evaluate two or three non-White groups. Particularly when ratings are organized into the subjective categories of most or least liked groups rather that into ethnic categories, one can see more clearly the evaluative distinctions they make between different groups. It is also interesting to note how similar is the liking for own and one other group among 8-year-olds. This may be one sign that early pervasive prejudice has disappeared though later selective prejudice may not have.

WHITE MAJORITY CHILDREN'S ATTITUDES TO WHITES

Although it is possible to assess prejudice toward ethnic groups independently of a preference for one's own, most studies have confounded one with the other. Regardless of this procedural problem, it is clear that both are an integral part of the child's developing attitudes.

To complete the picture, it will be important to present the findings with respect to attitudes toward one's own group. The results to be described revolve around answers to questions of whom one would want to play with and who has positive qualities.

There is some disagreement as to whether 3- and 4-year-olds show a strong preference for White peers. Asher and Allen (1969), Renninger and Williams (1966), and Vaughan (1964) report that they do; whereas others (e.g. Brown and Johnson, 1971; Katz and Zalk, 1974; Lerner and Buehrig, 1975; Rohrer, 1977) report that they do not. However, it is clear that by 4 and 5 years of age White children prefer their own group over Blacks (Aboud, 1980; Asher and Allen, 1969; Brown and Johnson, 1971; Crooks, 1970; Friedman, 1980; Greenwald and Oppenheim, 1968; Hraba and Grant, 1970; Kircher and Furby, 1971; Lerner and Buehrig, 1975; Morland, 1966; Renninger and Williams, 1966; Rice, Ruiz and Padilla, 1974; Vaughan, 1964). There are many more studies of children from 5 to 7 years of age, and these studies confirm that White children consistently prefer other Whites, that this preference may intensify during these early years, and that this preference is strong regardless of whether the alternative is a Black, an Asian, an Hispanic or a Native Indian (Aboud, 1977; Brown and Johnson, 1971; Clark et al., 1980; Corenblum and Wilson, 1982; Fox and Jordan, 1973; Goldstein et al., 1979; Gregor and McPherson, 1966a; Gregor and McPherson, 1966b; Hunsberger, 1978; Klein et al., 1979; Madge, 1976; Marsh, 1970; Milner, 1973; Morland and Hwang, 1981; Williams and Morland, 1976). Certain factors to be discussed more fully later reduce this White preference. For example, children of this age who were tested by a Black or Native Indian examiner often preferred the race of their examiner (Corenblum and Wilson, 1982; Katz and Zalk, 1974). However, Clark et al. (1980) found that the examiner's race did not affect such young children; only children who were in the concrete operational stage of development gave neutral rather than White biased responses when tested by a Black examiner. Another interesting factor is having a Black sibling. White British children who had a Black foster sibling preferred a Black peer over a White one (Marsh, 1970). Interestingly, the Black siblings had a reciprocal preference for a White peer. Except for these variations, White children showed a strong preference for their own group from a very early age.

Contrary to popular and professional belief (Brand et al., 1974), the attachment to one's own group does not consistently increase as the child grows older. Studies reveal that it did strengthen in some children between 4 and 7 years (e.g. Asher and Allen, 1969; Brown and Johnson, 1971; Clark et al., 1980; Hraba and Grant, 1970; Vaughan, 1964;

Williams et al., 1975), even in those who were already expressing a bias at 4 or 5 years. In other samples, the children's attitudes seem to remain stable and high throughout these early years (Aboud, 1977, 1980; Friedman, 1980). However, in many samples of children a discontinuity occurred in the 7 to 8 year age bracket. Around this age, children's single-minded preference for their own group began to erode and their attitude neutralized. For example, 3- to 11-year-old children were asked by Brown and Johnson (1971) to assign positive and negative adjectives to White and to Black peers. The percentage of positive adjectives assigned to Whites at first increased from 51 per cent at 3.5 years to a high of 78 per cent at 8.5 years and then decreased to 62 per cent at 10 years. The watershed age in this sample was 8.5 as it was in the children tested by Williams et al. (1975). In other samples, the peak occurred a year or so earlier. The precise age is not as critical as the cognitive (Clark et al., 1980) and individual factors (Friedman, 1980) that are associated with the subsequent decline. It is apparent that in addition to age variation, there is also a great deal of individual variation. Certain children over 7 years express more neutral attitudes after 7 years whereas other children do not (Epstein et al., 1976; Genesee et al., 1978; George and Hoppe, 1979; Katz et al., 1975).

This phenomenon was described previously when we examined how prejudice toward other groups changed with age. Recall that prejudice was lower in children older than 7 years. Because certain measures confound ingroup attachment and outgroup rejection, they prevent us from separating the two phenomena.

Only a few studies which have measured ingroup attitudes independently allow us to separate the phenomena. Stephan and Rosenfield (1979) asked 10- and 11-year-old children to rate Whites, Blacks and Hispanics separately along 10 bipolar adjective scales. The children described their own group more positively than the two other groups, as expected. However, all three groups appeared very close to the midpoint indicating that the older children evaluated their own group and other groups neutrally. Similarly, in the Aboud and Mitchell (1977) study, 8-year-olds liked their own group slightly less and liked three other groups more than 6-year-olds. We concluded that around 7 and 8 years of age, White children continue to prefer their own group but their attachment moderates. At the same time, they become more positive toward other groups. Kalin (1979) found that these two trends continued through childhood and adolescence. As yet we do not know whether one change triggers another or whether they are both reflections of the same underlying progression toward greater flexibility (Davey, 1983; Doyle, Beaudet and Aboud, 1987).

BLACK MINORITY CHILDREN'S ATTITUDES TO OWN AND OTHER GROUPS

Black children appear to form attitudes around the same age as Whites, that is by 3 or 4 years of age (Asher and Allen, 1969; Kircher and Furby, 1971). However, with a few exceptions, the pattern of ingroup attachment and outgroup rejection is typically not found among young Blacks. There is really no typical pattern before 7 years of age. Black children appear to be very heterogeneous in their ethnic group preferences. Some samples are pro-Black, others pro-White, and the majority of samples are split with some children being pro-Black and some pro-White. Thus, there are differences across samples, and there are individual differences within samples. The factors responsible for these differences are not frequently isolated, but will be discussed in chapter 5. After 7 years of age, Black children tend to be more attached to their own group and more negative toward others. It is not clear whether this attachment moderates later on during adolescence (Cross, 1980).

These conclusions are based on my review of 36 studies conducted over the last 20 years on Black children in North America, Britain and South Africa. In all three regions, Blacks are in a minority or less powerful position than Whites, a factor that presumably has a profound influence on their attitude development. These studies will now be described more fully.

Six of these investigations, testing children between 5 and 7 years of age, reported a preference for Blacks and a rejection of other groups (Aboud, 1980; Banks and Rompff, 1973; Goldstein et al., 1979, in their integrated sample only; Hraba and Grant, 1970; Lerner and Buehrig, 1975; Semaj, 1980, especially on the affect scales). Semaj, for example, asked children to rate Blacks and Whites separately on 10 affect scales. Whites were evaluated rather neutrally from 4 to 7 years of age, while Blacks were evaluated positively, particularly at 6 and 7 years. On the Preschool Racial Attitude Measure, which requires children to choose a Black or White for a series of evaluative descriptions, attitudes were not pro-Black until 6 years and were not strongly so until 8 years.

Banks and Rompff (1973) examined attitudes in an unusual way. One of their measures was based on personal evaluation and yielded a pro-Black attitude; a second measure was based on reward and yielded a pro-White bias. They showed the children two basketball players, one Black and one White, playing five trials of 'basketball'. Each won one trial by a large margin, won one trial by a small margin and tied one trial.

Therefore, they performed equally overall. After each trial, the children rewarded each player with candies. At the end, they nominated an all-round winner. Blacks chose the Black player as the all-round winner. However, they tended to give more rewards to the White player when he won by a large margin, compared to the Black player when he won similarly. The children appeared to treat evaluation and reward differently. Their overall evaluation appeared to be based on a personal bias, whereas reward seemed to be influenced by social value. Perhaps the children rewarded according to a combination of performance plus social status (the additive or augmentation effect is well known among attribution researchers, Sedlak and Kurtz, 1982). The extra factor they may have been considering, namely social status, could reflect their knowledge of social attitudes rather than their personal attitude. In any case, the discrepant attitudes expressed by children here point to a differentiated and perhaps unintegrated set of attitudes. Some would say that Blacks have positive attitudes toward both Blacks and Whites and that this is functional when one is simultaneously a member of a predominantly White society and a member of a Black ethnic group (e.g., Hraba, 1972). Others would say that the lack of consistency across measures reflects an ambivalence about one's own group. We discussed a type of ambivalent attitude previously with respect to White children. After 7 years of age, White children were more willing to see negative qualities in Whites along with the positive, and to see positive qualities in Blacks along with the negative. This ambivalence in White children is viewed as mature because it is thought to reflect a certain emotional and cognitive flexibility. In contrast, the ambivalence expressed by Blacks is often viewed as maladjustive because it is thought to reflect a lack of strong attachment or a lack of certainty about one's attachment. Perhaps because developmental psychologists do not expect to see cognitive flexibility at such an early age, they interpret the ambivalence as uncertainty. It may, however, be a form of flexibility that stems from social adaptability.

Similar conclusions could be drawn from the 16 studies where there was no strong preference for Blacks or no pro-Black consensus among the children. The 3- and 5-year-old children in Spencer's (1982) study, for example, scored around the midpoint on the Preschool Racial Attitude Measure. That is, overall they assigned positive and negative qualities to Blacks and to Whites about equally. This was true for both personal preference items and for social evaluation items. An example of the former is: 'Here are two girls. One of the girls would make a very nice playmate. Which one would you choose as a playmate?' An example of the latter is: 'Here are two boys playing. Everyone says how ugly one boy is. Which is the ugly boy?' Children in other studies similarly gave neutral or nonbiased responses on the PRAM (Branch and Newcombe, 1980; Semaj, 1980; Williams et al., 1975; Womack and Fulton, 1981). In studies using the Doll Technique, children also tended to be split in their choice of the Black or White doll as 'the good doll' or the one they would most want to play with. Results using this technique are expressed in terms of the percentage of children choosing the Black doll. Percentages around 35 per cent to 65 per cent indicate a lack of consensus among the children in their preferences (Bagley and Young, 1979; Branch and Newcombe, 1980; Fox and Jordan, 1973; Greenwald and Oppenheim, 1968; Gregor and McPherson, 1966a; Katz and Zalk, 1974; Klein et al., 1979; Milner, 1973; Moore, 1976; Morland, 1966; Morland and Hwang, 1981; Morland and Suthers, 1980; Rohrer, 1977; Simon, 1974; Williams and Morland, 1976).

How are we to interpret these neutral scores? Is there indeed no bias in children whose mean score is say 13 out of 24 on the PRAM? It is quite possible that some children scored in the pro-Black direction, some in the pro-White direction and some in the unbiased region. To answer this question we must look at the scores of individual children. Spencer (1982) provided results for each of these three categories. The figures were 16.5 per cent pro-Black, 57.4 per cent pro-White and 26 per cent no bias. Likewise, Rohrer (1977) found that 29 per cent preferred Blacks, 31 per cent preferred Whites and 39 per cent preferred Hispanics. Thus, although the overall group score appears to be neutral, in actuality some children are pro-Black, some prefer Whites and only a quarter are nonbiased.

Children under 7 years in other studies were largely biased in favour of Whites (Asher and Allen, 1969; Clark and Clark, 1947; Crooks, 1970; Goldstein et al., 1969, segregated sample; Gregor and McPherson, 1966b; Kircher and Furby, 1971; Madge, 1976; Morland, 1966, Southern sample; Newman, Liss and Sherman, 1983; Rice et al., 1974). For example, in the Asher and Allen (1969) study, 73 per cent of the children chose the White puppet to play with at 3 and 4 years; the percentage went up to 80 per cent at 5 and 6 years. Most of them chose the Black puppet as the bad one. Similarly, the Black kindergarten children in Newman et al.'s (1983) study preferred Whites and Hispanics equally over Blacks. These children were shown drawings of peers from the three ethnic groups in pairs and asked to choose which one they would like as a friend. Out of two paired comparisons, Black–White and Black–Hispanic, they chose the Black an average of 0.8 times, that is, less than half the time. They rejected the Black as often when he was paired with an Hispanic as when paired with a White child.

Children between 7 and 10 years are more consistenty biased in favour of Blacks than younger children are. In only one study, Black children appeared to prefer Whites over Blacks (Rice et al., 1974). Out of 12 published studies, 6 showed pro-Black attitudes (Davey, 1983; Epstein et al., 1976; Katz et al., 1975; Semaj, 1980; Stephan and Rosenfield, 1979; Ward and Braun, 1972). For example, 82 per cent of the 7- and 8-year-old children in Ward and Braun's (1972) study chose the Black puppet when asked which one had the nice colour; 79 per cent chose the White puppet as the bad one. Similarly, the average PRAM score for 8- and 9-year-old children in Semaj's (1980) study was 8.2 out of 12, up from 5.8 at 4 and 5 years. When Spencer (1982) extracted personal preference items from the PRAM, she too found a more pro-Black preference in 9-year-olds than in 5-year-olds, who were on average nonbiased. Interestingly, animal colour preferences became more pro-White and social values became slightly pro-Black. Other samples of children present a mixed picture with some children preferring Blacks, some Whites and some both equally (Asher and Allen, 1969; Newman et al., 1983; Spencer, 1982; Williams et al., 1975; Williams and Morland, 1976).

Whether the children appear pro-Black or split probably depends on their attitude in the early years. This is because there is good evidence that Black children become more pro-Black after 7 years (e.g. Asher and Allen, 1969; Newman et al., 1983; Semaj, 1980; Spencer, 1982; Williams and Morland, 1976). Thus, those who were pro-White in the early years probably shift toward the neutral point, and those who were neutral shift toward the pro-Black end. There is even some evidence that those who were already in favour of Blacks may begin to moderate their attitude back toward the neutral point (Semaj, 1980). Semaj found a decline in pro-Black attitudes from 8 to 10 years. However, it seems to be the case that once the major shift in attitude has taken place, there is little change over the next few years (Epstein et al., 1976; Katz et al., 1975; Williams et al., 1975).

My developmental interpretation here goes beyond the data in the sense that it is based on cross-sectional rather than longitudinal age comparisons. No longitudinal studies have been reported that allow us to follow a group of children from 5 to 9 years of age, and to note changes over that age span. The only longitudinal study to be reported (Branch and Newcombe, 1986) followed children for two years from 4–5 to 6–7 and found no changes over that range. The endeavour was laudable, but should be continued for another two years before predicting any significant change.

When Black children adopt a preference for Blacks, their attitude toward Whites does not necessarily become rejecting. Researchers who looked at the two attitudes independently of one another found that the children became neutral rather than negative toward Whites (Aboud, 1980; Davey, 1983; Semaj, 1980; Stephan and Rosenfield, 1979). For example, on 10 affect scales, the children in Semaj's study (1980) rated Whites at the midpoint. Black children in Stephan and Rosenfield's (1979) study rated Whites at the midpoint and Hispanics slightly lower. Similarly, those in Davey's (1983) study rated Whites neutrally and Asians considerably lower. Thus, they did not reject Whites, but they did hold negative attitudes toward another ethnic minority group.

The interpretation of this pattern of Black children's attitudes is not straightforward. Firstly, there is the issue of why Blacks do not consistently prefer their own group in the early years – after all, both they and their families are Black. Secondly, there is the issue of heterogeneity, because some prefer Blacks and some prefer Whites or Hispanics.

Concerning the first issue, it is clear that the problem of prejudice is not as striking with Blacks as it is with Whites until the children become a bit older. If anything, the problem is an early 'misplaced' attachment to a group other than their own, notably to Whites. This is an issue that we will confront again when discussing the attitudes of other minority children such as Asians, Hispanics and Native Indians. Their attitudes seem to reflect social values about which race is dominant rather than the physical reality of who they are. The self-identification process involved in knowing and understanding one's ethnicity is generally weak in these early years and may be distorted in line with attitudes. Misidentification often follows from 'misplaced' attachment, but then becomes corrected at 5 or 6 years when perceptual and cognitive processes mature. Ingroup preference follows shortly thereafter at 7 years. Thus, when attempting to explain unexpectedly low rates of own-group preference among minorities one must understand that early preferences are not constrained by the reality processes of self-perception and cognition. In these early years, motivations and emotions seem to dominate the child's life.

Concerning the second issue, it is surprising to find so much heterogeneity in children so young who are not yet exposed to many of the variable social forces present in our society. One possible explanation is that community and parent attitudes vary widely and that children adopt their parents' attitudes (Barnes, 1980). However, the evidence presented in a later chapter indicates that parental attitudes as such are not adopted by children of this age, though they may be reinterpreted by the child and so be influential in an altered form.

A more complete explanation for pro-White attitudes and for the heterogeneity of Black children's attitudes must await our discussion of the development of self-identification and the factors that contribute to attitude development.

OTHER MINORITY CHILDREN'S ATTITUDES TO OWN AND OTHER GROUPS

Hispanic children in the United States seem to follow the Black model in that they are heterogeneous in their preferences up to 7 years of age and then become more pro-Hispanic afterwards. For example, young Hispanic children in two studies preferred a Hispanic peer over a White peer (Newman et al., 1983; Rohrer, 1977). In two other studies, they preferred the White peer over an Hispanic (Rice et al., 1974; Weiland and Coughlin, 1979). Werner and Idella (1968) found a mixture of preferences in their sample which could be explained in terms of whether the child attended school or not. Children of 4 and 5 years of age who did not yet attend school preferred the Hispanic doll (75 per cent), whereas those who attended school preferred the White doll (85 per cent). The former group presumably had little exposure to Whites because they lived in a homogeneous neighbourhood, whereas the latter were interacting daily with White teachers. Exposure to White adults may be a very significant factor in the early years. However, with increasing age and school experience, Hispanic children from 7 to 10 years were found to become more pro-Hispanic (Newman et al., 1983; Rice et al., 1974; Stephan and Rosenfield, 1979), not pro-White. As with the Blacks, their attitudes toward Whites were not strongly negative, though their attitudes toward Blacks were (Newman et al., 1983; Rohrer, 1977; Stephan and Rosenfield, 1979).

Asian children's attitudes are not well documented in the research literature. The term Asian includes children with Chinese, Japanese, East Indian and Pakistani ancestry. Although these groups are not culturally similar, they have been combined for the present discussion because their attitudes tend to be similar and because there is too little research on any one group to treat them separately. Of the five studies reviewed, Aboud (1977) found a preference for White peers, Fox and Jordan (1973) and Milner (1973) found a relatively neutral score (which could mean that children are equally split among pro-Asian, pro-White and no bias), and two studies found a preference for their own Asian group. These two studies were different from the first three in that one of them was conducted with children in Taiwan and Hong Kong (Morland and Hwang, 1981) and the other was conducted with older children from 7 to 10 years (Davey, 1983). What we know so far about Asian children's attitudes is that they are mixed or pro-White in the early years, perhaps becoming more pro-Asian after 7 years, and are rejecting toward Blacks (Aboud, 1977; Davey, 1983; Milner, 1973).

Native Indian children are if anything more favourable toward Whites than are children from the previously discussed ethnic groups. Rosenthal (1974) claims that 3- and 4-year-old Native Indians show no consensus in their preference; however, from 4 years on, the children consistently express a strong preference for White peers (Corenblum and Annis, 1987; Corenblum and Wilson, 1982; George and Hoppe, 1979; Hunsberger, 1978). The only occasions when Indian children have expressed positive attitudes toward their own group was when attitudes toward many groups were assessed. Aboud (1977; Aboud and Mitchell, 1977) asked for separate evaluations of Indians, Whites, Blacks, and Hispanics or Asians. Under these conditions, children 6 years and older expressed liking for their own plus one other group and dislike of one or two other groups.

SUMMARY OF EMPIRICAL FINDINGS

The development of ethnic attitudes, in particular prejudice, can be summarized using the four questions outlined at the beginning of the chapter.

Question 1 At what age are ethnic attitudes first acquired? Ethnic attitudes are acquired by most children sometime between the ages of 3 and 5 years. The age of 4 is probably a safe bet if one wanted to pick a single age at which children express negative reactions to certain ethnic members. Whether the negativity is directed toward their own or other ethnicities depends to a certain extent on the child's own ethnic membership. White children are consistently negative toward members of another group. Of the minority groups discussed here, only Native Indians were consistently more negative to their own group than to Whites. The other minority children – Blacks, Hispanics and Asians – were more heterogeneous in that some were initially more negative to their own ethnic members.

Question 2 How do attitudes change thereafter during the preadolescent years? Between the age of 4 when attitudes are acquired and the age of 7, White children become more consensually and/or strongly biased against others and in favour of their own ethnic members. Minority children remain split over which is the negative and which the favoured group up to 7 years of age.

Ethnic minority children after the age of 7 and before adolescence less frequently express negative attitudes toward their own group. The usual pattern is either a bias against other groups and in favour of their own or a more neutral/nonconsensual attitude toward their own and others. White children, in contrast, either show no change in their outgroup prejudice during this preadolescent period, or show a decline in prejudice while maintaining a less intense preference for their own group.

Question 3   Is prejudice toward other groups related to favouritism toward one's own group? It is currently difficult to answer this question because of a limitation in the tests used. This limitation is found whenever children are required to express their attitude by choosing only one ethnicity in response to a question. Because the two or three groups have not been evaluated separately, rejection of one group is confounded with acceptance of another group. On the basis of studies which allow for independent evaluation, it would seem that to a certain extent own and other group attitudes are inversely related.

Question 4   Do attitudes toward one's own and other groups differ for majority and minority children? Yes, they do, particularly in the early years from 4 to 7 when White majority children are more strongly and consensually biased in favour of their own and against other groups. They become more similar by 10 years of age when most children show a preference for their own over others. At this age, individual children within majority and minority groups differ in the extent to which own and other group attitudes are polarized or neutralized. What differences do exist are probably due to the actual or perceived social status of the child's group. Because almost all the studies reported here were conducted in stratified societies where Whites have higher status, I have referred to the White group as the 'majority' and to the other ethnic groups as the 'minorities'.

4 The Development of Ethnic Awareness and Identification

Ethnic awareness refers to the conscious recognition of race or ethnicity in individuals and groups. Some people believe that being aware of ethnicity leads to prejudice. So they try to discourage children from noticing that people look different, that people have different shades of skin colour, different eyes or different ways of talking. This merely serves to discourage an accurate perception of reality. In fact, people are different in many ways just as they are similar in many ways. Furthermore, there is no clear evidence that race and ethnic awareness does lead to prejudice. Certainly, to be prejudiced one must first notice the differences for which one develops a dislike. However, unprejudiced children also notice these same differences. They simply do not react negatively to them.

For many reasons, however, it is important to know at what age children first become aware of ethnic and racial differences and how this awareness expands toward a deeper understanding of ethnicity and race. One reason is that awareness is a necessary precursor of attitude formation whether positive or negative. A second reason is that awareness feeds into and is fed by the child's growing self-identification. In the process of trying to know more about themselves, children increase their knowledge about others. One might expect that attitudes develop in line with self-identification, that the child develops a preference for those who are seen as similar. However, in the case of minority group children, this is not so, as their early preference is often for Whites. At a certain age their awareness and self-identification become realistic and accurate. Still their preference may be for another group. This not uncommon discrepancy between whom one identifies with and whom one prefers is interesting because it suggests that the process of identification and attitude formation can follow divergent paths. Eventually, however, they seem to come together for most children.

Once again, because of the large amount of research available on this topic, I found it useful to focus on a few theoretically relevant questions.

1 At what age do children first show their awareness of different ethnic groups?
2 How does the awareness of ethnicity change with age, become deeper and more complex with age?
3 How does the awareness of one's own ethnicity change with age?
4 Does ethnic awareness and self-identification differ for majority and minority children?
5 Is the development of ethnic awareness related to prejudice?

This chapter will concentrate firstly on the development of ethnic awareness and then on the development of ethnic self-identification. The research findings indicate that awareness of others' ethnicity and of one's own seem to follow a similar course of development, beginning firstly with the correct application of an ethnic label, then with perceptions of similarity to members within a group and dissimilarity to members from different groups, and lastly with categorization and cognitions about the meaning of ethnic affiliation.

AWARENESS OF THE ETHNICITY OF OTHERS

Applying an ethnic label correctly or identifying which person goes with a given ethnic label is usually measured by showing pictures or dolls from different ethnic groups and asking the child to point to, for example, the White, the Black and the Native Indian person. A significant proportion of children make correct identifications at 4 and 5 years of age and this proportion increases with age. By 6 and 7 years the children reach close to 100 per cent accuracy especially when identifying Whites and Blacks. Two studies found that 3-year-olds were very inaccurate in that less than 25 per cent of them correctly pointed to the White and Black when given those labels (Renninger and Williams, 1966; Williams and Morland, 1976). However, 4- and 5-year-olds reached close to 75 per cent accuracy or better in both White and Black samples (Clark and Clark, 1947; Crooks, 1970; Greenwald and Oppenheim, 1968; Katz and Zalk, 1974; Rice et al., 1974; Williams and Morland, 1976). Most of these studies also indicate a significant improvement with age, suggesting that 3 to 5 are the critical years for acquiring this form of label awareness. By improvement, I mean that a larger proportion of children made accurate identifications. Older White and Black children of 6, 7 and 8 years usually reached a level of 90 per cent to 100 per cent accuracy (Epstein et al., 1976; Fox and Jordan, 1973; Friedman, 1980; Gregor and McPherson, 1966a; Gregor and McPherson, 1966b; Weiland and Coughlin, 1979; Williams and Morland, 1976).

According to Fox and Jordan (1973), it is also between the ages of 5 and 7 years that White and Chinese Americans acquire the ability to identify Chinese people. However, the identification of Hispanics or Mexican Americans seems to be more difficult for both White and Hispanic children. They improved in accuracy between 4 and 9 years of age and reached asymptote around 9 or 10 years (Rice et al., 1974; Weiland and Coughlin, 1979). Similarly, the identification of Native Indians by both White and Indian children was fairly good by 6 years of age but continued to improve during the next 3 years (George and Hoppe, 1979; Hunsberger, 1978; Rosenthal, 1974). Presumably the children were using features such as skin colour and hair type for Whites and Blacks (Kircher and Furby, 1971) and so found Hispanics, Indians and Whites less distinctive in these features than Whites and Blacks.

The child's awareness of ethnic groupings also takes the form of perceiving certain similarities between members of the same group and perceiving certain differences between members of different groups. Vaughan (1963) gave children sets of three pictures of people and asked them which two were similar and different from the third. By 6 years of age the children had reached a level of 68 per cent accuracy and this improved to 83 per cent by 11 years. Similarly, Katz et al. (1975) asked children to rate the degree of similarity between pairs of people. At 8 years of age, White and Black children rated same-ethnic pairs as more similar than different-ethnic pairs. That is, two Whites were perceived as very similar and two Blacks were perceived as very similar despite their different facial features or different shades of skin colour. Black children rated two Whites as slightly more similar than two Blacks. However, a White and a Black were always perceived as very different. An interesting result from the Katz et al. study was that in later years, perceptions of dissimilarity were not always based on race but were sometimes based on individual features such as emotional expression. In other words, the children had acquired perceptions of racial similarity and difference by 8 years, had continued to use these perceptions for the following three years, and then abandoned them at 11 or 12 years in favour of perceptions of individual features. Thus, we must keep in mind the fact that racial awareness is often overused when it is first acquired, but that it may lose its salience later on when other types of awareness become more useful.

Another method was used by Aboud and Mitchell (1977) to examine how children perceive similarities and differences among different ethnic members. The Native Indian children in this study were first asked to place photographs of men from four different ethnic groups on a similarity board to indicate how similar the men were to themselves. Then a peer from each ethnic group was placed (one at a time) at the end of the board. The children were asked to repeat the rating procedure, this time to indicate how similar the men were to each ethnic peer. The children, who ranged from 6 to 10 years of age, accurately perceived the same-ethnic man as most similar to the peer and the three different-ethnic men as equally dissimilar. On a second task, they were asked whom each ethnic peer would most want as an uncle or brother. It was expected that these kinship selections would closely parallel the similarity ratings as indeed they did.

When White children of the same age were given the same task they made a number of interesting errors. Younger children often made egocentric errors in that they assigned the uncle they wanted, a White uncle, to another ethnic peer. Both younger and older children also made mismatch errors in that they assigned an incorrect non-White uncle to the peer. These mismatches were especially frequent when the peer came from a disliked ethnic group, or when the peer, whether from their own or a disliked group, spoke his non-English native language (e.g., the Asian child spoke Chinese, the Hispanic Spanish and the White French). Perceptions of ethnic similarity or kinship received interference both from the child's own strong preferences and from his or her strong dislikes. It seemed that the older children were able to control their own strong preferences but not their dislikes. The errors for the disliked group were probably due to a lack of knowledge or attention to details. Johnson, Middleton and Tajfel (1970) also found that children possessed least knowledge about national groups that they disliked. This lack of knowledge or attention to detail has manifested itself in several different ways. For example, in the Aboud and Mitchell (1977) study, many children chose the wrong, but not their ingroup, ethnic uncle. In the Middleton et al. (1970) study, it was reported that British children from 7 to 11 years were egocentric in suggesting that a disliked outgroup peer would prefer a British person. The opposite was found by Genesee et al. (1978) where more ingroup preference or ethnocentrism was attributed to disliked nationalities. The egocentric judgements of British children support Piaget's observations of Swiss children, but not the reports of North American children. Perhaps egocentrism persists longer when one is assigning preferences to national groups with whom one has little contact rather than ethnic groups living in one's community.

Vaughan (1963; 1987) found that children were able to categorize by race and to give appropriate labels to people only after they were relatively accurate at perceiving similarities. He claimed that categorizing and labelling required certain cognitive skills, such as classification, that matured later than perceptual skills. For example, Vaughan asked children to sort White and Maori dolls by race. At 5 and 6 years of age, only 60 per cent of the children could do this correctly. However, by 7 years of age 85 per cent of the children were accurate, and 100 per cent were at 8 years. Similarly, when Vaughan showed them a doll and asked 'What sort of doll is this?' not until 7 years of age did a significant proportion of the children give the correct racial label: 85 per cent at 7 years of age and 100 per cent at 8 years.

Other researchers have used the sorting task but they have used it to measure the salience of race over other cues such as sex and age rather than as a measure of awareness of categories. Madge (1976) and Davey (1983) presented children with pictures of people who varied in race, sex and age. The children sorted these pictures into two boxes of people who 'belong together'. Almost half the children sorted the people according to race; this was true for White, Black and Asian children who ranged from 6 to 10 years of age. Sorting by race increased with age for the White children only. Given Vaughan's data, we cannot be sure whether the younger children sorted by sex or age because they were unable to sort by race or because sex and age were more salient to them. However, the older children were presumably capable of sorting by any one of the categories but chose race because it was the most salient. We might expect then that sorting by race or ethnicity increases from 4 to 7 years as children develop a cognitive awareness of racial categories. Whether it increases or decreases thereafter depends on the other categories available. Relative to sex and age, race remained salient for Davey's (1983) children. However, relative to personality or individual features, race became less salient for the White children in Katz et al.'s (1975) study.

A more mature form of ethnic awareness involves understanding that race and ethnicity are tied to something deeper than clothing and other superficial features. Adults think of a person's ethnicity as being derived from his or her family background. However, young children are not aware of this deeper meaning of ethnicity; they are fooled by superficial features. For example, not until the age of 9 or 10 do Black children seem to be aware that a person remains Black even though she puts on white makeup or a blond wig, or even though she may want to be White (Semaj, 1980; Vaughan, 1963). This deeper awareness manifests itself in many ways. One of these is constancy or the constant identification of a person's ethnicity despite transformations in superficial features. Aboud (1984) examined constancy by showing children a photograph of an

Italian Canadian who was labelled as such. Then a sequence of four photos was shown of the Italian Canadian boy donning Native Indian clothing over the top of his ordinary clothes. In the final photo, the boy's appearance had changed except for his face. The children were asked to identify the boy in the final photo. Constancy was said to be present if the child said that he was Italian and not Indian (label), that he was more similar to photos of other Italian children than to photos of Indians (perceived similarity), and that he should be put into the pile of other Italians (categorization). Constancy increased from 5 to 9 years of age but was not really present until 8 years (see table 1). Most children younger than 8 years thought the boy was Indian.

Furthermore, when asked if the boys in the first and last photos were the same person or two different persons, half the 6-year-olds said they were two different persons. Over 90 per cent of the 7-year-olds knew they were the same boy, but not until a year later did they attain ethnic constancy. Children of 8 years and older were certain that the boy was Italian and not Indian. Consistent with our previous discussion, the two cognitive identifications of labelling and categorization were more difficult than the perceived similarity identification. At 8 years they not only identified the boy as Italian but also inferred that he would prefer an Italian over an Indian playmate. However, although the 8- and 9-year-olds understood that ethnicity was deeper than clothing, they were not able to articulate the reason for this. When asked what makes a person Italian or Indian, only a few mentioned country of birth or family but most did not know.

Another manifestation of children's maturing awareness of ethnicity is that they understand the cause of skin colour. Clark, Hocevar and Dembo (1980) tested the notion that with age children dispense with their early view that skin colour is caused supernaturally or through

Table 1   Mean scores on constancy and related measures (range of possible score in brackets)

Response measure		K	Grade 1	Grade 2	Grade 3
Composite constancy score	(0 to 3)	0.60	1.17	2.56	2.10
Perceived sameness of first and fifth photo	(0, 1)	0.50	0.92	1.00	1.00
Inferred preference	(0, 1)	0.30	0.58	0.89	0.80
Basis of ethnicity	(0 to 2)	0.10	0.33	0.56	0.60
Conservation	(0 to 4)	1.10	2.25	2.88	3.30

arbitrary association (e.g. being American or being bad) and begin to understand that it is transmitted via a physical mechanism from parents to children. Children were asked, 'How is it that this person is white . . . this one black?' Their answers were coded in terms of 7 levels of understanding the cause of skin colour. Children became aware that there were physical origins of a person's skin colour after the age of 7, though they did not make the link to parents till some time later. Understanding the physical basis of skin colour was acquired after they had mastered conservation. This awareness developed around the same time as identity constancy, measured here as the understanding that kinship remains constant despite a change in age and family size. It is clear, then, that ethnic constancy and a mature understanding of skin colour are later developments and require a fairly mature level of cognitive development. Clark et al. (1980) also found that this level of awareness was necessary for the decline in White children's prejudice toward Blacks.

AWARENESS OF ONE'S OWN ETHNICITY

The identification of one's own ethnic background closely parallels the awareness of other persons' ethnicity. It is not clear which comes first, although there are reasons for believing that self-identification develops more rapidly. That is, once children acquire the initial recognition of ethnic groups, they proceed through the levels of self-identification rapidly. For example, Vaughan (1963) found that children accurately perceived the ethnic similarity between themselves and another child a year or two before they accurately perceived similarities among others. However, there are so few data on the latter that no firm conclusions can yet be drawn.

Many researchers assess awareness of one's own ethnicity by asking children to point to the picture or doll that looks most like them. This measure emphasizes appearance, though the child is presumably free to consider any feature of appearance such as skin colour or hair or body weight. British White children as young as 3 years of age have been found to identify with the White person or doll with a frequency of 75 per cent (Marsh, 1970). Except for this one study, most researchers have tested children 4 years and older. White children of 4 and 5 years typically identified with their own group 70 per cent to 80 per cent of the time (Crooks, 1970; Fox and Jordan, 1973; Greenwald and Oppenheim, 1968; Marsh, 1970; Morland, 1966; Morland and Hwang, 1981; Newman et al., 1983; Rice et al., 1974; Rohrer, 1977; Vaughan, 1963;

Williams and Morland, 1976). By 6 and 7 years, almost 100 per cent of the children said they were similar to the ingroup person (Aboud, 1977, 1980; Corenblum and Wilson, 1982; Fox and Jordan, 1973; Friedman, 1980; Gregor and McPherson, 1966a, 1966b; Marsh, 1970; Milner, 1973; Newman et al., 1983; Vaughan, 1963) though not in all studies (Davey, 1983; Simon, 1974; Weiland and Coughlin, 1979; Williams and Morland, 1976). Regardless of the absolute levels of accuracy or percentage of children claiming ingroup similarity, most studies report significant improvements between 4 and 8 years of age indicating that identifying oneself in terms of similar appearance is present in a significant majority of children by 4 or 5 years and increases over the next 3 years (Aboud, 1977, 1980; Fox and Jordan, 1973; Genesee et al., 1978; Marsh, 1970; Newman et al., 1983; Vaughan, 1963).

Although many researchers obtain data on both self-identification and ethnic attitudes, very few examine whether the two are related. Looking at the results for each measure separately, one notes that self-identification scores are generally higher than preference scores. In only three studies were self-identification and preference scores equivalent (Crooks, 1970; Vaughan, 1963, 1964; Williams and Morland, 1976). However, the majority of studies found that more children from 4 to 7 years said they look like the White than said they prefer the White (Corenblum and Annis, 1987; Corenblum and Wilson, 1982; Fox and Jordan, 1973; Gregor and McPherson, 1966a, 1966b; Marsh, 1970; Morland, 1966; Newman et al., 1983; Rice et al., 1974; Rohrer, 1977; Simon, 1974). In other words, some children said that they looked most like the White but preferred the Black as a playmate. Similar skin colour may provide the basis for most children's attitudes but not for all. It is conceivable that some children base their preferences on other perceived or inferred qualities such as play activities or facial expression. In fact, very few researchers have been able to tell us what attributes are salient for perceived similarity because they specify a priori that the attribute be appearance. When children are asked who *is* most similar to them, they are less likely to choose the White person. Aboud (1977, 1980) found that only 57 per cent of 5- and 6-year-olds chose a White, though this jumped to over 75 per cent among 6- and 7-year-olds. The basis for choice was most frequently an inferred behaviour and secondly an aspect of appearance unrelated to ethnicity. Likewise, behaviour and appearance may be most salient to a young child when making preference judgements.

Another important dimension that has been neglected in this research is the child's perception of dissimilarity. According to research to be described more fully in chapter 5 (see Rosenbaum, 1986), prejudice arises out of a dislike for differences, not out of an identification or perceived similarity to one's own group. Because the perceived similarity measure is usually based on a choice of one person, it is assumed that the rejected person is perceived as different. This may not be so. The rejected person may be seen as slightly less similar than the chosen person, yet not as different. Alternatively, they may both be seen as different but the rejected person as more so. There is some evidence that ethnicity may be more salient when deciding who is different from oneself, and other features such as behaviour more salient when deciding who is similar. McGuire, McGuire, Child and Fujioka (1978) found that children more often mentioned ethnicity when asked, 'What are you not?' than when asked, 'What are you?' Similarly, Aboud (1977) found that ethnicity was more often given as a reason why someone was different than why someone was similar.

Black children also begin to identify with other Blacks around the age of 3 years in that some of them choose a Black doll or photo as looking most like themselves. However, whereas 8 of the 12 studies using 75 per cent of the samples of White children found significant White identification between the ages of 3 and 5, only 6 of the 15 studies of Black children did. Again, the youngest group of children tested were 3 years of age and 76 per cent of them said that they looked most like a Black child (Marsh, 1970). Greenwald and Oppenheim (1968) also found that 79 per cent of their 3- to 5-year-old Black sample identified with either the Black or the mulatto doll. In three other samples of 4- and 5-year-olds, the children identified with a Black (Fox and Jordan, 1973; Morland, 1966; Rohrer, 1977, integrated Blacks). However, most others have found that Black children of 3 to 5 years of age did not in significant numbers say they looked like the Black child. By this, I mean that less than 70 per cent of the children chose a Black as looking most like them, the approximate figure for statistical significance given most of the sample sizes (Crooks, 1970; Gregor and McPherson, 1966b; Morland and Hwang, 1981; Morland and Suthers, 1980; Newman et al., 1983; Roberts, Moseley and Chamberlain, 1975; Rohrer, 1977; Simon, 1974; Williams and Morland, 1976). Thus, during these early years a large number of Black children do not perceive themselves to look like other Blacks. There are significant increases each year, but the biggest changes seem to take place around 5 and 6. By 6 and 7 years of age, the proportion identifying with Blacks is close to 80 per cent. Even among older children the figure rarely exceeds 90 per cent (Davey, 1983; Epstein et al., 1976; Fox and Jordan, 1973; Gregor and McPherson, 1966a, 1966b; Milner, 1973; Morland and Suthers, 1980; Newman et al., 1983; Rice et al., 1974; Roberts et al., 1975; Williams and Morland, 1976).

Similar findings were obtained by Schofield (1978) using two different measures. She asked Black children of 6 to 8 years to select pictures of themselves within a school and within a family context. For example, one context was a playground scene with pictures of two Black boys, two Black girls, two White boys and two White girls. The children were told to position all the pictures on the playground as if it were recess, and to identify which one was himself or herself. The family context consisted of two men, two women, two boys and two girls, one Black and one White of each. The children were told to identify representations of their family members. This technique provides a familiar and realistic context to elicit the child's self-identification. Many of the children identified themselves as the White child. Interestingly, the scores on this test correlated with scores on the Draw-a-Person test where children were asked to simply draw a person with crayons. White children generally drew a person with yellow or peach skin colour and blond or brown hair. Black children often drew a White person (44 per cent), or left the race of the person ambiguous (30 per cent); only 24 per cent drew a Black person. The underlying assumption here is that the child of 6 or 7 years will spontaneously draw himself or herself when asked to draw 'a person' and so the colours chosen will reveal their self-identification. Correlations with the more controlled picture choice test support this assumption.

As mentioned previously, little is known about whom Black children perceive themselves to be different from. This is particularly important given that many children do not choose the Black as most similar. Does this mean that they see the Black as different? This question cannot be answered with the measure usually used by researchers. When children do not choose the Black person, they could be saying that he/she is different or that he/she is similar but not most similar. The only way to resolve this issue is to allow children to rate the degree of dissimilarity between themselves and others (Aboud and Mitchell, 1977). Another somewhat less than optimal way was used by Aboud (1980) who showed the children pictures of three Blacks and asked if each were similar or different. Black children between 5 and 7 years answered that one or two were similar and the third was different from them. Incidentally, White children also responded this way to their ingroup members. When asked the same about three members from each of four non-Black groups, the Black children saw these other groups as being for the most part different. With age, Black children saw themselves as similar to more Blacks and different from more non-Blacks. Interestingly, liking was positively related to perceived difference, i.e. the more non-Black differences they saw, the more positive was their attitude to these non-Blacks.

As I described previously for White children, the self-identification scores of young Blacks are sometimes higher than their preferences for Blacks. In fact, in many cases, Blacks between 4 and 7 years perceived themselves as similar to other Blacks but did not prefer them (Clark and Clark, 1947; Fox and Jordan, 1973; Greenwald and Oppenheim, 1968; Gregor and McPherson, 1966b; Marsh, 1970; Morland, 1966; Rohrer, 1977; Simon, 1974). The discrepancy between identity and preference is very striking in these studies. In almost an equal number of samples, identification with Blacks and preference for Blacks are both low and equivalent (Crooks, 1970; Morland and Hwang, 1981; Morland and Suthers, 1980; Newman et al., 1983; Roberts et al., 1975; Williams and Morland, 1976). From this one might conclude that before the reality-oriented processes such as perception and cognition have matured, identification may be influenced, even determined, by emotions and preferences. However, when reality-based processes develop sufficiently, they seem to determine self-identification but to have no effect on preferences, at least for several years. Between the ages of 7 and 10, Black children's preferences come into line with their self-identification as Blacks.

The self-identification of Asian Chinese children as measured through their perceptions of similarity to other Chinese is also frequently absent before 7 years. Only half of the children at 4, 5 and 6 years of age said they looked most like the Chinese child (Fox and Jordan, 1973; Morland and Hwang, 1981). Many of these children said they were most similar to a White child. When given the option, up to half said they looked like neither Chinese nor White targets (Morland and Hwang, 1981). Aboud (1977) tested Chinese Canadian children at a Chinese preschool and found that almost half felt most similar to a White and a third most similar to an Indian, Eskimo or Black, leaving less than 20 per cent who saw themselves as most similar to a Chinese child. Surprisingly, an equal proportion said they were most different from a White and from an Indian, Eskimo or Black. The children were either sticking with the same ethnic group and basing their same–different judgements on individual features, or were switching ethnic groups and basing their judgements on dark–light colouring. However, by 7 and 8 years, over 75 per cent of Asian children said they looked most like an Asian (Aboud and Christian, 1979; Davey, 1983; Fox and Jordan, 1973; Milner, 1973). As with the Black children, Asian children seem to reach an asymptote of 85 per cent or 90 per cent at 7 or 8 years and to show no further increases with age after this point.

Similarly, Hispanic children are evenly split in their identification with Hispanics and Whites at 4 and 5 years of age. Approximately half said they were most similar to another Hispanic and half said they were most similar to a White person (Rice et al., 1974; Rohrer, 1977; Werner and Idella, 1968). At 6, 7 and 8 years, over 80 per cent identified with an Hispanic person (Newman et al., 1983; Rice et al., 1974; Weiland and Coughlin, 1979).

Native Indian children seem to identify with Whites or with Whites and Indians equally from 5 to 7 years of age and right up to 10 years of age (Aboud, 1977; Corenblum and Wilson, 1982; George and Hoppe, 1979; Hunsberger, 1978; Rosenthal, 1974). At 10 and 11 years, a significant proportion of around 70 per cent perceived themselves to be similar to another Indian. Indian identification has been found to increase greatly when the children are tested by an Indian adult rather than a White (Corenblum and Annis, 1987; Corenblum and Wilson, 1982). We have also found Indian identification among 6- and 7-year olds who were asked to rate the degree of similarity between themselves and many different ethnic members. They rated themselves more similar to an Indian than to a non-Indian person, even one they liked, though not as similar as White children did to their group (Aboud and Mitchell, 1977). Thus, although the existing literature suggests that Indian self-identification occurs late in childhood, there is some evidence that they may be no different from other minority groups in that identification is present but not strong at 7 years.

Previously, we discussed more mature, cognitive forms of ethnic awareness such as knowing ethnic labels, grouping people into ethnic groups and understanding that ethnicity remains constant. Very few of these measures have been used to measure ethnic self-identification. Thus, it is not clear whether these various forms of self-identification are acquired together or sequentially. For example, it is not known whether children learn their ethnic label before or after they perceive their similarity to ingroup members. On the one hand, children could learn their ethnic label before 2 years of age just as they learn their name and gender. In this case, we would not want to infer any special understanding of ethnic group membership from this achievement. On the other hand, labelling oneself correctly could mean that they are going beyond the perception of individuals and attributes, and understanding that they are part of a large group. If the latter is true, knowing one's label and knowing how to group oneself will develop after perceptions of similarity and difference.

Aboud (1980) examined this issue using a Guttman scalogram to determine the sequence of acquisition. Children were offered five ethnic labels one at a time and asked to indicate whether the label applied to them or not. White children knew their label earlier than Black children. The Blacks knew their correct label only if they already perceived themselves to be similar to other Blacks, whereas some Whites had acquired their label before the perceived similarity and some after. Thus, Black children appear to learn their label as a second step in the self-identification process, perhaps as a result of noticing similarities and differences. Some Whites appear to learn their label as a second step, and some as a first step before it has any grounding in perceptions of similarity.

The results of another study (Aboud, 1977) suggest that the label measure may more accurately reflect the self-identification of minority children. If they do not know their label, they usually deny that any label applies rather than choose the wrong one. However, children may perceive themselves as similar to an outgroup member yet know their correct label. For example, many Native Indian and Chinese 5- to 7-year-old Canadians said correctly that they were Indian or Chinese but did not perceive themselves as similar to members from that group. Conversely, many perceived themselves as similar to a White but few said they were White. These discrepancies are partly due to the different basis of each judgement, one the perception of features and the other knowledge of one's label. They point out that unlike White children, minorities often hold what appear to be inconsistent or discrepant ideas though in fact they may not be incompatible. These perceptions may be as crucial as the child's self-identification in determining prejudice.

SUMMARY OF EMPIRICAL FINDINGS

The development of ethnic awareness and self-identification can be summarized in terms of the four questions outlined at the beginning of the chapter.

Question 1 At what age do children first show their awareness of different ethnic groups? Children first show their awareness at 4 and 5 years of age when a significantly large proportion of them can accurately point to people who are White and Black. This is true of most children regardless of their own ethnicity. However, their recognition of Native Indians, Chinese Americans and Hispanics is delayed by a few years, perhaps because the distinctive features of these groups are less salient.

Question 2 How does the awareness of ethnicity change with age? Firstly, children become more accurate at correctly identifying people from different ethnic groups when given the ethnic label. Secondly, other more complex forms of awareness develop, namely perceptions of within-group similarity and between-group differences, and cognitions about ethnic constancy. Perceptions of similarity and dissimilarity between individual ethnic members follow ethnic lines at a later age, between 6 and 8 years. Sorting into ethnic categories and labelling often do not become accurate until 7 years. When children become aware of ethnicity, they tend to overuse it in their perceptions and categorizations. However, with age children often attend less to ethnicity and more to attributes related to the individual. The understanding that ethnicity is not based on superficial features and that it is constant is acquired around 8 years of age.

Question 3   How does the awareness of one's own ethnicity change with age? In selecting the picture or doll which looks most like them, most White children reveal a White identity at 4 years of age; the number reaches almost 100 per cent by 6 and 7 years. The percentage of Black and Hispanic children who select an ingroup member is slightly lower at 4 years but again asymptotes around 6 and 7 years. Asian children do not show significant ingroup perceived similarity till 8 years and Native Indians often later still, according to published studies. Knowing one's ethnic label may be learned early, simply as a linguistic tag, or learned later as a social category to which one belongs. There are two currently unresolved issues arising out of a comparison of the perceived similarity and the label measures. One is a question about the sequence of their development. A second is whether the label measure is a more accurate index of minority children's ethnic identification.

Question 4   Does ethnic awareness and self-identification differ for majority and minority children? There is no evidence that majority and minority children differ in the age at which they acquire the various forms of ethnic awareness. However, their ethnic self-identification does differ. White children perceive themselves to look similar to an ingroup member earlier than Black and Hispanic children who catch up by 7 years. Asian and Native Indian children develop this response somewhat later. There is no evidence that labels or constancy responses develop later in minority than in majority children.

Question 5   Is the development of ethnic awareness related to prejudice? Being aware that different ethnic groups exist, though not necessarily being accurate in identifying them, clearly precedes prejudice. However, it does not determine prejudice in that both prejudiced and unprejudiced children are aware of ethnicity. It seems more likely that ethnic self-identification affects preference and perceived difference affects prejudice. These two relationships will be discussed more thoroughly in chapter 7. However, the data described here reveal that between 4 and 7 years of age, while these judgements are being acquired, many children identify with their ingroup but prefer an outgroup. This is true not only of minority children, but also to a certain extent of White majority children.

5 Critical Examination of Design and Measures

The studies described in chapters 3 and 4 have many glaring limitations. The purpose in raising these weak points is twofold. Firstly, readers must be cautioned that conclusions drawn from the research are limited by the samples, designs and measures used. A simple example is that children from many national and ethnic groups have not been tested or are not included in this review. They may hold strikingly different attitudes (see Lambert and Klineberg, 1967). Limitations of this sort potentially limit the validity of explanations of prejudice that are based on such data. Secondly, researchers have been slow to improve upon their designs and measures. Methodology developed sometimes 40 years ago is still being used unchanged, without regard for new theories that could be tested or new, psychometrically stronger measures. This is not to say that the data obtained with these methods are inaccurate, but rather that a more complete and credible database could be had.

Seven limitations of this research will be critically examined. Some deal with the measures used, specifically with their reliability, validity, target stumuli and response alternatives. Others deal with matters related to design and the ability to test various theories.

TEST–RETEST RELIABILITY AND INTERCORRELATIONS BETWEEN MEASURES

Test–retest reliability is an important psychometric property of any test. It indicates the extent to which a test can measure the same quality at two points in time and come up with a similar score. With measures of childhood prejudice, researchers have been lax in providing this information. Moderate group reliability over a 1-year time period has been reported for only two measures: the Preschool Racial Attitude Measure or PRAM II (Williams and Morland, 1976) and the Katz–Zalk

Projective Prejudice Test (Katz and Zalk, 1978). Reliability over a longer period of time is not reasonable to expect given what we know about the developmental aspects of prejudice. However, like other phenomena such as cognitive differentiation (measured by the Embedded Figures Test) which reflect both stable individual differences and developmental change, we might expect that children remain stable relative to their peers but change as a group.

Intercorrelations between different measures of prejudice are important because they indicate whether prejudice is a unitary construct or is different depending on the context. Katz et al. (1975) found low intercorrelations between scores from the Projective Prejudice Test, the Intolerance Scale, the Dogmatism Scale and a measure of Social Distance. However, the Intolerance and the Dogmatism Scales do not, strictly speaking, measure ethnic prejudice. Rather, they measure aspects of social thought that theoretically might underlie prejudice or be associated with it. Apparently, in children they are unrelated to prejudice. We could not conclude from this that prejudice is not a unitary construct; it may not yet have become integrated with other reactions. The Social Distance measure described by Katz is not frequently used, so at this point little can be said about its usefulness. Branch and Newcombe (1986) gave three prejudice measures to two age groups and found that four of the six correlations were significant, though only in the 0.30 range. The three measures were the standard Clark Doll Technique, a modified Doll Technique which allowed for multiple doll choices on any item, and the PRAM. One could conclude that prejudice is a unitary construct but that test scores may differ depending on the number of items and range of responses allowed. This will be discussed more fully shortly.

VALIDITY: DO THE TESTS MEASURE PREJUDICE?

The measures used to assess prejudice or attitudes are valid only if they actually measure what they are supposed to. Criterial validity is determined by correlating an attitude with its related behaviour. For a long time, measures of adult attitudes were considered invalid because they did not relate to behaviour. The problem has recently been traced to two factors, the simplicity of the measure and the personality of the respondent (see Jackson and Paunonen, 1980). With respect to the first, scores based on aggregated responses to items varying in context and form correlate more highly with behaviour than do single-item scores. Secondly, individuals differ in the extent to which attitudes guide their behaviour. So-called high self-monitors who use social cues in the setting to guide their behaviour show less attitude–behaviour consistency than low self-monitors who use internal beliefs and attitudes. Like the former group, children may express variable responses not because the measure is poor but because they use context cues rather than internal states to guide their responses.

Many researchers have turned to the use of friendship measures in place of attitude tests (e.g. St John and Lewis, 1975; Singleton and Asher, 1979; Whitley, Schofield and Snyder, 1984). They claim that friendship is an important factor in reducing prejudice and in school achievement (Damico, Bell–Nathaniel and Green, 1981; Pettigrew, 1967). Others feel that friendship is a more valid index of attitudes than is a test. The latter claim is questionable. Two studies compared the ethnicity of the preferred doll or photo with the ethnicity of the child's friends (Davey and Mullin, 1980; Hraba and Grant, 1970). They found that peers from other ethnic groups were more frequently friends than they were preferred hypothetical playmates. The choice of a friend, however, is determined by more than simply one's attitude to that person's ethnicity; other attributes of the friend such as common interests are important. Friendship choice is therefore not a substitute for a good test of attitudes. Other behavioural measures such as amount of voluntary contact with an unfamiliar person might be better for validating an attitude test. The attributes other than ethnicity can be controlled in this case.

The transparent purpose of most attitude measures is a problem that bears on their validity. The objection here is that respondents inhibit their expression of prejudice in order to appear socially desirable. Older children in particular may be aware that the questions measure prejudice; they may also be more sensitive to which attitudes are socially approved. This awareness is said to account for the decline in prejudice among White children over 7 years (Katz et al., 1975).

At issue is whether older children have altered their responses or actually possess a more positive underlying predisposition toward other groups. In support of the response–alteration hypothesis, some researchers have found that children express less prejudice in the presence of an outgroup examiner than an ingroup examiner (Clark et al., 1980; Corenblum and Wilson, 1982; Friedman, 1980; Katz et al., 1975; Katz and Zalk, 1978). Temporary differences such as this one, which are due to the context, are interpreted as evidence that the children consciously alter their responses, not their dispositions. However, our discussion of this phenomenon in chapter 6 points out firstly that the effect of the examiner's ethnicity is not widespread or consistent, and secondly that different factors explain the effect when it appears in different age groups. In young children with a high need for approval, the desire to please the examiner may induce them to change their responses temporarily. In older children, the examiner's ethnicity may serve as a cue to prime certain weak cognitions about respect and about the similarities of different ethnic groups. These cognitions are important in changing the child's underlying predisposition toward ethnic groups.

Independent of the effect of the examiner's ethnicity, the problem is whether social desirability leads to response alterations. This problem has been tackled by comparing the responses to tests which differ in the transparency of their purpose. Verna (1982), for example, claims that social desirability did not affect responses on his social distance measure or his conflict index to the same extent that it does on a forced-choice test. Another strategy used by Doyle et al. (1987) is to measure the social desirability concerns of children as well as their assumptions about what attitudes would be considered desirable by the examiner, i.e. what attitudes were held by the examiner. As expected, social desirability scores as measured by the Social Desirability Scale for Children (Crandall, Crandall and Katkovsky, 1965) declined between 6 and 12 years of age. Secondly, children at each grade level expected the examiner's attitudes to be more prejudiced than their own. These results do not support the idea that children inhibit their prejudice in order to be seen as socially desirable by the examiner. Given their perception of the examiner, they should have expressed more prejudice to obtain approval. An alternative explanation is that children projected their own more prejudiced attitudes on to the examiner; in this case, their actual level of prejudice was slightly higher than what was expressed but nonetheless declined with age.

The question of whether a test of prejudice is valid cannot be answered simply. The two criteria discussed here are the minimization of extraneous factors such as social desirability, and the relation with behaviour considered to be expressive of prejudice. The assessment of extraneous factors and the choice of an appropriate behaviour has not always been easy. Few tests of prejudice have been evaluated against these two criteria. Clearly, it is possible to find tests that are less transparent measures of prejudice and thus reduce the intrusion of extraneous factors (Katz et al., 1975; Verna, 1982). It is also possible to find tests that have been correlated with behavioural manifestations of prejudice (Stephan and Rosenfield, 1979). In the future, more tests need to be evaluated for their validity.

THE USE OF STIMULUS DOLLS, PHOTOGRAPHS AND CLASSMATES

Most of the early studies and many recent ones used dolls to represent different ethnic group members. The rationale was that, like all projective materials, dolls minimize the fear of retaliation and thus elicit uninhibited feelings. This strength, however, is outweighed by more serious limitations. Dolls do not represent people the child would meet; they are toys to be manipulated; they are often sought out because they are familiar; and they have a different meaning for younger and for older children. Since 1974 most studies have used pictures of peers in order to avoid the limitation of dolls. Although the results with young children using dolls seem to be comparable to those found using pictures, more appropriate comparisons can be made with children over 6 years if all studies use the picture format. Photographs in particular allow for variation in the features commonly found in a group of people, whereas dolls do not. Averaging across the ratings made toward several representatives of the same ethnic group incorporates this response to variation. It also eliminates the possibility of having only one ethnic representative who unintentionally differs on an extraneous feature, such as attractiveness. With these advantages, plus the obvious need to include stimulus persons for whom dolls are not readily available, pictures are better than dolls for the assessment of attitudes.

Drawings can be used to eliminate extraneous factors such as attractiveness. The PRAM, for example, requires children to choose between pairs of people who are identical except for the colour of their skin. Strictly speaking, the test measures attitudes to skin colour rather than to ethnic groups. The people with dark skin colour appear to come from any of a number of ethnic groups: East Indians and Native Indians, as well as Blacks. So far, it has been used with children who assume that the people are Whites and Blacks because skin colour is the cue used to categorize these groups. For broader use with other minority groups, such as Native Indians, Doyle and I have had to change the drawings so that hair style as well as skin colour differs (see figure 4).

In some studies, the researchers have used classmates as the stimulus persons. The attitude questions are asked and children respond by choosing someone from their class. The ethnicity of the classmate is then used to score responses. Unfortunately, classmates are too well known to use in the assessment of ethnic attitudes. The attitude toward a classmate will be determined largely by the classmate's personality and only partly by the classmate's ethnicity (Whitley, Schofield and Snyder, 1984).

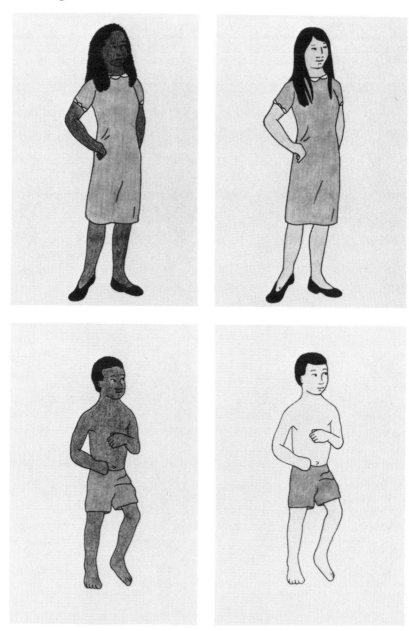

Figure 4   Modified drawings used with the PRAM and developed by Doyle and Aboud (Black and Native Indian girls; Black and White boys)

Consequently, these attitudes toward specific and known people do not generalize to other members of the group. In this sense, they do not constitute ethnic attitudes.

THE NUMBER OF OUTGROUPS INCLUDED

Most researchers have assessed attitudes toward only two ethnic groups, the child's own group and a so-called outgroup. Because of this limitation and the use of forced-choice responses, children appear to like one group and dislike the other. In fact, children sometimes like more than one ethnic group and sometimes dislike more than one (e.g. Aboud, 1981; Aboud and Mitchell, 1977; George and Hoppe, 1979). This finding is inconsistent with the dichotomy of an ingroup and an outgroup, and points out the need to determine which perceived qualities of a group make them liked or disliked. That is, in addition to explaining why children hold negative attitudes at all, we might also want to understand why they dislike that particular ethnic group. The former is the goal of authoritarian and cognitive developmental theories; the latter is a goal of social reflection theories.

Three outgroup qualities thought to provoke prejudice are social value, conflict (Sherif and Sherif, 1969) and dissimilarity (LeVine and Campbell, 1972). Social value is the major determinant of prejudice according to social reflection theories. The social value of a group is its perceived status or power in the society. The idea is that when societies are stratified, power is unequally distributed. Power may be based on numbers alone, but more likely on political and economic control. When status differences are recognized and accepted by most members of society, there will be general consensus on each group's social value. The particular groups to be disliked, then, are the ones with low status and value in the society.

Conflict between groups can affect attitudes through one of several mediators. The conflict may entail frustrating competition in which one frequently fails to attain limited resources or a desired goal. The frustration then leads to aggression which is directed at the perceived source of the frustration, namely the competing ethnic group. A second possible mediator of conflict is the within-group cohesion and between-group distance that accompanies conflict. Members and particularly children belonging to groups in conflict may have more within-group contact and so develop more familiarity and attachment to their group. At the same time, they become less familiar with the outgroup. Distance and lack of familiarity could therefore be the cause of prejudice between groups in conflict. A third possible mediator is the perception of threat from a conflicting outgroup and the feeling of security one receives from one's own group. Fear and insecurity generated by the threatening outgroup could account for the development of negative attitudes toward them. The fear of strangers one sees so frequently in children during their second year is often attributed to the threatening qualities of a stranger, particularly one who comes too close. Thus, although the conflict itself may not be apparent to young children, mediating factors such as frustration, unfamiliarity or threat may be attached to certain groups more than to others, and so arouse prejudice.

Another quality thought to affect prejudice is dissimilarity. Groups who are perceived as different from oneself are generally disliked more than outgroups perceived as similar. Dissimilarity may affect attitudes for a number of reasons, the most likely being that dissimilar people are assumed to hold different values, preferences and beliefs from self. I will refer to these judgement differences as disagreements because I feel they are different from and more powerful than differences in external appearance. Disagreement in particular may be disconcerting because it is seen as an invalidation of one's own beliefs. To the extent that people seek validation of their beliefs from other people and avoid invalidation, they will avoid dissimilar groups.

Children tend to react more intensely than adults to differences and disagreement. Two studies demonstrate their negative evaluation of disagreers. Enright and Lapsley (1981) asked children to evaluate peers who expressed opinions different from their own, such as whether a boy should help his friend with homework against the wishes of his teacher. Nine-year-olds thought that these peers were wrong and were generally bad people. Twelve-year-olds were sometimes just as negative, although an equal number said that the disagreeing peers were good or that nobody was wrong. In this case, younger children were more negatively affected by disagreement and generalized their evaluation of the peer's opinion to the peer as a person. The Enright and Lapsley study looked at disagreements between children from the same ethnic group. It is inevitable that peers from different ethnic groups will disagree or assume they will disagree on many things, one being their ethnic preferences. In one study (Aboud, 1981), I examined how 5- to 9-year-old children reacted to peers who disagreed with their preferences. After the children had laid out five photos on a liking board to show how much they liked each ethnic member, they saw a mirror image set of preferences from a member of the ethnic group they least liked. Would they understand that the two different preferences were both valid and reasonable because they came from two different perspectives? Only 33 per cent of the children were able to reconcile the different preferences, to allow that both were valid because they reflected the preferences of different ethnic members. The proportion of children reconciling the difference increased with age (it jumped to 66 per cent in a subsequently tested sample of 9- to 12-year-olds). Younger children were therefore more negatively affected by the disagreement in that they assumed that one person was wrong, either themselves or the peer. A second reaction was also found among 8- and 9-year-olds. The disagreement forced them to reconsider their own judgements. Regardless of their evaluation, they were subsequently found to change their own preferences in line with those of the peer. These two studies demonstrate clearly that younger children are more intensely affected by disagreement than older children, in that disagreement implies a negative evaluation of either oneself or the disagreer, or that disagreement exerts pressure to change one's preferences.

Limiting stimulus persons to only one outgroup not only creates the erroneous impression that all outgroups are evaluated similarly, but also leads to another false conclusion. This is the conclusion that Whites are more rejecting of other groups than are minority children (Brand et al., 1974). Usually, minority children are asked to express their attitude toward their own group and Whites. Because so many of the 4- to 7-year-olds prefer Whites, they are assumed to show little rejection of outgroups. The problem is that non-White outgroups are rarely evaluated. The few studies that have included them indicate that minority children do express prejudice. For example, Native Indians strongly rejected Blacks in one study (George and Hoppe, 1969) and expressed dislike toward three out of four outgroups in another study (Aboud and Mitchell, 1977). Davey (1983) reported that Blacks in Britain disliked Asians and Asians disliked Blacks. Thus, prejudice is not solely a White phenomenon. Although Whites are clearly more favourable toward their own group than are Black and non-Black minorities, they may not be more rejecting of other groups.

FORCED CHOICES *VERSUS* INDEPENDENT RATINGS

Most of the reported studies have asked children to choose one of two stimulus persons with whom they would like to play or who is the good one. There are three problems associated with this technique. One is that the forced choice includes no index of intensity. For example, the unchosen stimulus may evoke a slightly less intense response than the chosen one (on a 10-point scale say the former evokes 5 and the latter 7), but it receives instead a zero score.

The second problem is that group frequencies are often interpreted as if they were the mean scores of a sample of individuals. Frequencies that do not differ from chance are interpreted as nonpreference (Banks, 1976), though in reality two sets of children may be expressing strong but opposite preferences. When the data show 60 per cent of Blacks in favour of their own group and 40 per cent in favour of Whites (a nonsignificant difference), this is taken to mean that Black children are equally in favour of Blacks and Whites, as if individual children had no strong preferences. A more accurate interpretation is that there is no consensus as to preferred ethnic group among the children in the sample; however, individual children may hold strong, polarized preferences. Forced choices allow one to determine only how many children show a preference, not how strongly the preference is held.

The third problem is that forced choices confound acceptance of one group with rejection of another group. When the children make their choice, they can be influenced by their attitude toward their own group or their attitude toward the other group or both. The response may reflect an approach toward the chosen stimulus or an avoidance of the unchosen one. The investigator cannot know which attitude is being expressed. The solution is to measure attitudes to each group independently. One technique is the continuous rating scale on which each group is rated separately in terms of how much one likes or wants to sit close to them (Aboud and Mitchell, 1977; Verna, 1982). Any number of groups can be evaluated independently this way, and the score indicates the intensity of the attitude. A second technique is to allow the children to choose any number of own and other group members who fit the evaluation (Doyle et al., 1987; Lerner and Schroeder, 1975). When asked, 'Who is smart?' children may choose up to five Blacks and five Whites, or any other group. The number of people chosen from each group is taken as an index of the intensity of the positive attitude, given a positive adjective, or the intensity of the negative attitude, given a negative adjective. A comparison of the results derived from forced-choice and independent rating procedures suggests that the discrepancy is essentially one of intensity. Rejected groups in particular may be evaluated less negatively on independent ratings scales.

An interesting theoretical question arising from this debate is the question of which attitude is more intense and which stimulus group more salient, the accepted one or the rejected one. There are two points of view here. Brewer (1979) claims that people distinguish themselves from others but do not distinguish among others unless they receive additional information about the other's group membership. This information serves only to enhance liking for those designated as ingroup members; it does not reduce liking for those designated as outgroup members. Thus, Brewer feels that the salient and more powerful information affecting one's attitude is about a person's ingroup status or similarity. Information that a person is from the outgroup does not strongly alter one's attitude from what it was before one received group information. This implies that attitudes develop and change because of a growing attachment to one's own group and not because of a change in prejudice toward other groups.

An opposing hypothesis is proposed by Rosenbaum (1986) who claims that dissimilarity information about outgroup status is the more salient item and that rejection and repulsion are the more salient attitudes. Rosenbaum considered attitudes to people described in non-group terms as a baseline. He found that the addition of outgroup information produced a greater change in attitude from the baseline than did ingroup information. In other words, people disliked those from the outgroup and their attitudes were considerably more negative than if they had received solely non-group information. In contrast, people were attracted to those from their own group but not any more so than if they had received solely the non-group information. Rosenbaum concluded that similarity is affectively neutral, whereas dissimilarity is affectively potent and aversive. This implies that attitudes develop and change because of a reaction to dissimilarity or inconsistency with what one expects.

Although the controversy seems to have been resolved in favour of the salience of outgroup status, the results might have been different had the research been conducted with children instead of adults. One might argue that because children between 4 and 7 years do not have a strong ethnic self-identification, they do not assume the ethnic status of a stranger. Thus, ingroup information is just as unexpected and novel as outgroup information. Also, baseline attitudes of young children may be more neutral or negative than those of adults because of their lack of experience or familiarity with strangers. A lower baseline would allow for more change in a positive direction. With children over 7 years, it is safe to assume that their reaction to outgroup members is more salient than their reaction to ingroup members, and that results of the forced-choice technique are primarily a measure of attitudes toward outgroups.

COHORT EFFECTS

Most of the research has examined age differences using a cross-sectional design in which children from different age groups are compared at one point in time. It is assumed that the attitudes held currently by the older group of children will be held by the younger ones several years down the road. Results from cross-sectional designs are often interpreted as if they applied longitudinally, that is, to the same children at two different points in time. One problem with cross-sectional designs is that the two groups differ not only in age but also in year of birth. Year of birth tends to coincide with temporal differences in societal influences which are known as cohort variables. Cohort variables arise from historical events that change the climate in which one grows up. They include social values, education experiences and child-rearing practices. Cohort variables could therefore account for some of the age differences reported.

Cohort variables may also explain the strikingly different conclusions of studies published before the mid-1960s in the United States. The studies showed that attitudes became more extreme with age: positive attitudes to the ingroup becoming more positive and negative attitudes to the outgroup becoming more negative (Brand et al., 1974). My own conclusion, based predominantly on the attitudes of children born after the Civil Rights Movement, is that White children become less ethnocentric with age or maintain the same level, and that Black children develop a favourable but not strongly biased attitude toward their own group. Because the samples represent different cohorts, the differences could be accounted for by any one of a number of cohort variables, such as the social undesirability of prejudice, and parent attitudes.

The best design procedure for separating age and cohort effects is the cross-sequential design, which samples age cross-sectionally and then follows each longitudinally, adding another sample of the youngest age at each testing (see Horn and Donaldson, 1976). Although it is not possible to isolate completely the effects of each variable, because of the confounding of time of measurement and test experience with age and cohort, this procedure is generally advocated (Adam, 1978). One recent study that did look at both cross-sectional and longitudinal differences found only cross-sectional ones, which imply cohort differences (Branch and Newcombe, 1986).

ATHEORETICAL OBJECTIVES

One very disappointing limitation of the research is the lack of any theory testing. The goal of most studies was simply to describe the attitudes of a sample of children. Often no attempt was made to compare the different age groups (even though the data were available), to correlate identification with attitude, or to examine the effects of other variables such as respondents' ethnicity, knowledge of social stratification or authoritarianism of parents. The relatively small number of studies that test the relation between theoretically interesting variables, such as authoritarian child-rearing, and prejudice in children will be discussed in chapters 6 and 7. However, the studies cited in chapter 3, whether specifically designed for the purpose or not, can be used to test theoretical predictions about prejudice as it relates to the age and ethnicity of the respondent.

Take, for example, predictions about the age at which prejudice first appears in children and how it changes thereafter. The research indicated that at the age of 3, and certainly by 4, many children express strong likes and dislikes for members of different ethnic groups. This disputes the claim of social reflection theories that children of 4 years are positive toward other ethnicities, and become negative only later after learning the prejudices of their parents and community. The research also indicated that children do not consistently become more extreme in their attitudes over time. Older children are not always more prejudiced than younger ones, as social reflection theories predict. We found instead that White children show an increase only between the ages of 4 and 7 years. After 7 years, their prejudice either remains at the same level as predicted by the authoritarian theory or it decreases as predicted by social-cognitive developmental theory. Minority children become more pro-ingroup and anti-outgroup with age, but because they tend to be pro-outgroup or unbiased when young, this change does not often result in highly polarized attitudes.

The research also indicated differences between White majority children who generally prefer their own group, and minority children who show more heterogeneity and more outgroup preference. The findings are not as simple as predicted by social reflection theories in that not all children prefer Whites and not all children prefer their ingroup. However, the first prediction does come close to describing the attitudes of children between 4 and 7 years; and the second prediction describes the attitudes of most post-7 children. Neither the authoritarian theory nor the social-cognitive developmental theory provides a satisfying explanation for ethnic differences in preference.

The purpose of these examples is to raise two theoretical issues, namely about age and ethnicity, which could have been explicitly addressed in most of the studies, but were not. If researchers had attempted to test theories, they might have been more careful about designing the study to include age groups and ethnic samples that are relevant for predictions.

SUMMARY OF RESEARCH LIMITATIONS

Seven limitations of the research have been discussed in this chapter. These limitations concern problems in measurement and design which limit confidence in, but should not negate the conclusions drawn about, age and ethnic differences in prejudice.

1 Test–retest reliability coefficients are available and reasonality high for only two measures, the PRAM II and the Katz–Zalk Test. Intercorrelations among measures of prejudice indicate that it is a unitary construct though scores may vary depending on the number of items in the test and the number of response alternatives.
2 The validity of a test of prejudice may be determined by correlating scores with a behavioural index such as voluntary contact. Problems associated with the evaluation of a test's validity include the use of a single prejudice item, the use of friend's ethnicity as a behavioural index and the interfering effects of social desirability.
3 The use of dolls and classmates as ethnic targets can confound the measure of ethnic attitudes with other factors. It was suggested that photographs and drawings, equated for attractiveness and other extraneous factors, be used because they are appropriate for older as well as younger chidren, and because they allow for generalization to members of the group.
4 Most studies include only the ingroup and one outgroup to be evaluated. Consequently, they are unable to document the possibility that children like more than one ethnic group and dislike more than one. This possibility raises two issues that need further examination. One is that only certain outgroups are disliked, and so researchers must identify what intergroup factors arouse prejudice (e.g., status, frustrating competition, lack of contact, unfamiliarity, threat and disagreement). The second issue is that minority children are often not prejudiced toward Whites but are prejudiced toward other outgroups. Prejudice is not solely a White phenomenon and must be explored in other groups as well.
5 A major problem is the use of forced-choice formats which confound acceptance of one group with rejection of another. In order to assess accurately children's attitudes toward both ingroup and outgroups and to examine the relationships between attitudes, they must be evaluated independently. Two strategies for doing this were discussed. One is to evaluate each group on a continuous rating scale, another is to make non-forced choices. Both strategies are compatible with the PRAM in

that they are alternative response strategies to be used with the PRAM evaluative items. A third issue is whether ingroup or outgroup attitudes are more intense and deviate more from a baseline.

6 The cross-sectional age design of most studies leaves them subject to the confounding of age with cohort variables. Longitudinal designs, in particular the cross-sequential design which combines both cross-sectional and longitudinal testing, overcome most of the problems.

7 Finally, there is a lamentable lack of theory testing in studies of children's attitudes.

6 Social and Psychological Determinants of Prejudice

Initially, three theories were offered to explain why children are prejudiced. Each emphasizes certain social and cultural factors and certain psychological factors that encourage the development of prejudice. Which of these three theories is the correct explanation? Are social values and conflicts internalized by young children as they listen to parents, teachers and the media? Do children displace and project their hostility toward their parents on to minority groups? Or is the development of prejudice an inevitable consequence of early cognitive limitations? After reviewing the empirical data describing the development of prejudice, it became clear that certain theories are better than others at explaining these data. For example, the social reflection theory is good at explaining why Whites are preferred by young children from both majority White groups and minority groups, in that their attitudes seem to reflect the values of their society. The social-cognitive developmental theory seems to be better at explaining why children's attitudes change around 7 or 8 years of age, in that major cognitive changes take place at this age.

Another strategy for deciding which theory is better is to examine specific factors thought to be influential in the formation of attitudes. For example, to examine the factor of parent values, researchers have adopted a correlational strategy in which they relate the child's level of prejudice to the parents' level of prejudice. This allows them to test the idea that children learn their attitudes from their parents. If children's prejudice does not correlate with their parents', then we must conclude that there is no evidence that children are adopting the attitudes they hear from their parents. If the two do correlate, then it is likely (but not certain) that children have learned their prejudice from their parents. It is not certain only because it is possible that some other factor, such as unresolved hostility, is present in both child and parent which in turn causes both to be prejudiced. Learning may in this case be irrelevant. Because of the complexities involved in discovering the causes of prejudice, it is not yet possible to say definitely that one theory is the right explanation. We can only say that one theory is better because it has more support.

This chapter will present the evidence for certain factors thought to be causes or determinants of prejudice. These factors relate to the first two traditional theories of prejudice, namely the social reflection theory and the inner state authoritarian theory. In particular, the factors of social stratification, contact and parental ethnocentrism relate most strongly to the social reflection theory because they deal with social norms about the value of various ethnic groups and the child's experience with stratification and group competition. The factor of parental child-rearing practices relates most strongly to the authoritarian theory because it deals with early family experiences that affect the child's repressed resentment toward authority and the child's self-esteem.

While examining the evidence with respect to social and psychological factors, it will be important to keep in mind two aspects of prejudice. One is that the level of prejudice varies as a function of the child's own ethnic background. White children consistently prefer their own group over others, and express prejudice toward many others. In contrast, minority group children show much more heterogeneity. Many of them prefer Whites over their own group, although this changes with age. One basic issue to be explained then is why majority and minority group children differ so much in their attitudes. Is it because of the status of these two groups, or because of their proportions in the society? The difference may also be due to a difference in their parents' attitudes or their teachers' attitudes. Another important aspect of prejudice to keep in mind is the fact that it changes with age, particularly around 7 or 8 years. Many White children become less prejudiced with age and become more neutral toward their own group. Many minority children become more positive toward their own group with age. Are these age differences due to learning or to cognitive advances? Ethnic background and age differences are therefore two aspects of prejudice that must be explained.

Five social factors and three psychological factors will be evaluated as determinants of child prejudice. By social factors I mean that they arise from the social situation, though they clearly have corresponding psychological representations. As a psychologist, I feel that the latter are more influential than the former. For example, for social status to have an impact on a child's attitudes, it must be represented cognitively or otherwise in the child's mind. The social factors include social stratification, contact in a multi-ethnic school, ethnicity of the examiner, parental ethnocentrism and parental authoritarianism. The psychological factors include self-esteem, need for approval and gender. Other psychological determinants that are relevant to social-cognitive developmental theory will be discussed in chapter 7.

SOCIAL STRATIFICATION

The term stratification is used to refer to general status differences that exist in the society between groups and to the degree of competition between groups. Morland and Hwang (1981) felt that first it was important to describe certain societies as homogeneous or heterogeneous with respect to the ethnic mix present in the society. China and Taiwan, for example, are described as homogeneous because most of the people living in those countries have a Chinese or Asian background. In contrast, North American and many European countries as well as Hong Kong are heterogeneous in that many ethnic groups coexist in these countries. Among heterogeneous societies, there are those that are stratified in that certain ethnic groups have higher status or power than others. This is typical of North American and European societies. Others are less stratified in that status differences do not parallel ethnic differences. Although some people have higher status than others, ethnic groups do not have higher or lower status. In comparing the attitudes of children from these different societies, Morland and Hwang (1981) found that the degree of stratification but not the degree of heterogeneity determined children's prejudice. Children from both Taiwan (homogeneous) and Hong Kong (considered heterogeneous and nonstratified) were much less prejudiced toward others and less strongly biased toward their own group than children from the United States which is stratified. In other words, heterogeneous societies did not have prejudiced children unless they were also stratified. Multi-ethnic differences did not in themselves produce prejudice. This is not fully supported by research conducted in other heterogeneous and stratified societies. Doyle et al. (1987) examined the prejudice of English Canadian children toward French Canadians, who in the city of Montreal hold positions of equal status. These children were prejudiced toward French Canadians, though the levels were lower in children over 8 years. These key factors of heterogeneity and status stratification have been examined in many ways and will come up again when we discuss other social factors such as children's knowledge of status differences and proportion of ethnic mix in the child's school.

Heterogeneity or ethnic mix is psychologically represented as social categorization. Tajfel (1978) claimed that people form ethnic categories in their minds and then categorize people into these groups. Indeed, we saw in chapter 4 that at a certain age children can accurately label and group pictures of people from different ethnicities. Tajfel further claimed that people use these ethnic categories to identify themselves when the association leads to self-enhancement. In the service of enhancing themselves, people develop a bias toward their own ethnic group and against other ethnic groups. If identification with one's ethnic group does not lead to self-enhancement because the group has low social status, then self-enhancement will be sought through individual reward and not through group prejudice. Turner's (1978) research findings supported this theory. He placed people into various groups and varied whether reward (i.e. enhancement) could be derived individually or through the group. He found that one's own group was always preferred over the other group, and that this bias was maximized when reward could be obtained only through the group. Similar biases were found among White New Zealand children aged 7 through 11 years (Vaughan, 1978). The children gave rewards to ingroup and outgroup members using a strategy that maximized the difference between what ingroup members and outgroup members received. They used a similar strategy when allocating rewards to their friends and nonfriends. Thus, when rewards are assigned to groups, children not only give more to the people with whom they are associated, but they maximize the difference between their associates and their nonassociates. In contrast, minority Polynesian children in New Zealand used a strategy which maximized the joint profit of both groups (Wetherell, 1982). That is, both groups were given a large and equal number of rewards.

Tajfel's theory might explain why children from high status groups show more prejudice than ones from lower status groups, because they can more successfully obtain self-enhancement through association with their group. But it does not explain why many lower-status children identify with and prefer the high-status group. On the basis of this theory, one would expect them to show no bias and to obtain self-enhancement through individual achievement. It is possible that in an ethnic context, their only means of self-enhancement is through association with a group other than their own. How and why minority-status children make this association is left unanswered. Because most of this research has been conducted with older children or adults, it cannot easily explain the associations or identifications made by children 7 years and younger.

In a further test of these ideas of ethnic categorization and identity, Moscovici and Paicheler (1978) proposed that a secure, enhancing identity could be derived from either belonging to a majority (numerous) group or receiving a positive self-evaluation that enhanced one's self-esteem. People were put into either a majority or minority group on the basis of whether many or few people shared their opinions. They were then given a positive or negative evaluation about their performance on a test. Bias toward their own and the other group was subsequently assessed. According to my reading of the results, strongest bias was shown by people who possessed a tenuous self-esteem, that is by people in the majority group with low self-evaluation and by people in the minority group with high self-evaluation. Lower bias was shown by people who possessed either a high, secure esteem because they belonged to the majority group with high self-evaluation, or a low self-esteem because they belonged to the minority group and received low self-evaluation. Presumably the people with a tenuous self-identity were attempting to derive some enhancement by identifying with and enhancing their group. People with a secure identity did not need to derive any more enhancement through group bias; and people with a negative identity were attempting to dissociate from the group that provided them with no enhancement. In summary, positive self-evaluation reduces the bias found in majority group members; whereas it increases the bias found in minority group members. To a certain extent, these findings mirror the attitude changes found after 7 years of age with majority White and minority Black or Indian children. After this age, White children who were initially strongly biased become less so, and Blacks and Indians who were initially not biased toward their own group become more so. Although an important psychological goal is to develop a secure and positive self-identity, steps toward this goal may initially raise ethnic bias.

Child's socio-economic status. Another strategy for determining the effects of social stratification on prejudice is to see whether prejudice is related to the child's socio-economic status (SES). In light of our previous discussion, one might expect that middle-class children would be more prejudiced than lower-class children because their ethnic-SES group would provide an avenue for self-enhancement. A more complex prediction could be derived from the findings of Moscovici and Paicheler (1978). Those with a tenuous identity, that is lower-class Whites and middle-class minorities, would be expected to show the most prejudice.

Unfortunately, the findings for children do not neatly fit either of these predictions. Vaughan (1964) found no SES differences for White children; regardless of class they were most prejudiced between 5 and 7 years and then became less so from 8 to 12 years. Black children often show no class differences in the early years (Branch and Newcombe, 1980; Ward and Braun, 1972). Minority children older than 5 years, however, do show class differences. Middle-class Blacks between 5 and 8 showed more prejudice than lower-class Blacks, but they were prejudiced toward their own group and preferred Whites (Asher and Allen, 1969). In another study, middle-class Blacks showed more preference for Blacks than did lower-class children, though they were not prejudiced toward Whites (Spencer, 1983). Middle-class Hispanics at 12 years of age were more prejudiced against Whites than lower-class Hispanics (Iadicola, 1983).

Thus, on the basis of these few studies, we might conclude that White children show prejudice regardless of their socio-economic status, whereas minority children are more affected by their class. They are not strongly affected in the early years possibly because they are not aware of class differences. In the next few years, their SES membership does seem to affect prejudice in the way predicted by Moscovici and Paicheler (1978) in that middle-class minority children are more prejudiced. But only the older middle-class children's prejudice is directed toward the outgroup Whites. The younger middle-class children may direct their prejudice toward their own minority group. This suggests that younger children are aware of status differences between ethnic groups, but are not aware of their own status until 12 years of age. Thus, one explanation of class differences rests on the child's understanding of his/her group's status in the community. Another explanation, to be discussed more fully later, focuses on the different attitudes held by parents from lower and middle SES groups. Middle-class Blacks may be more pro-White because their parents are themselves integrated into White society and favour integration for their children.

Child's knowledge of social stratification. An important question to raise at this point is at what age children understand the ethnic stratification of their society. Using a multidimensional scaling technique, Aboud and Christian (1979) examined how children at 8 and 10 years of age categorized five ethnic groups in their society. The children came from Jewish, Chinese and Greek Canadian families. One of the main divisions was ingroup versus outgroups. Another division seemed to be based on skin colour. By using these two criteria, children appeared to categorize the groups in terms of their social status; however, the categorization was based on simple and concrete criteria rather than political and economic criteria. We can see from this that by 8 years of age children might have ways of categorizing various ethnic groups in simple terms.

However, learning the social status or value of these ethnic groups is a more complex affair. According to a large study by Rosenberg and Simmons (1971), minority children do not become aware of the lower status of their group until they reach the age of 12 or possibly earlier if they attend a multi-ethnic school. The researchers asked Black children between 8 and 18 years who 'most people would think is best'. Almost two-thirds (63 per cent) of the children between 8 and 11 years thought that most people would think Blacks were best. The number declined sharply after 11 years. When asked what class their family belonged to, again the younger children overestimated their family's SES. The authors make the point that most working-class Blacks live in a homogeneous environment, and their comparisons are with Blacks who are similar to them. Children who live in a middle-class community or attend a multi-ethnic school where there is more heterogeneity make more comparisons with Whites and with higher-status people. Such comparisons might lead to perceptions of inferiority. By 12 years of age, children regardless of their environment become aware of the larger society and its stratification. Their judgements of status then reflect their actual status within the larger society.

The question remains as to whether minority children's knowledge of their group's status affects their attitude toward their group. Because Rosenberg and Simmons did not measure ethnic attitudes, they were unable to answer this question. However, we might juxtapose what we know about the attitudes of Black children from chapter 3 with these findings on status knowledge to suggest some possible answers. Recall that Black children older than 7 or 8 years were somewhat pro-Black. They did not all prefer Blacks; the percentage approximated to or was slightly higher than the 63 per cent who said that most people thought Blacks were best. Thus, the children's perception of the social value or status of their group coincides with their own perception of who is best. Recall that one of the important factors influencing children's perception of their group's status at this age was whether they attended a racially mixed school. We will examine this factor more carefully in the next section.

How can the low ingroup preference of younger Black children be explained in terms of status knowledge? Although Rosenberg and Simmons did not ask younger children about the status of Blacks, they would probably infer that children between 4 and 7 years are even more likely to live in a homogeneous Black environment than are children between 8 and 11 years. Thus, more than 63 per cent would be likely to say that people think Blacks are best. This does not coincide with the small number of children who prefer Blacks over Whites. One would have to conclude that perception of Black status does not explain the attitudes of Black children from 4 to 7 years. Some other factor must be operating at this age. Conversely, children older than 11 years perceive

Blacks to have low status in the society, but their attitudes tend to be pro-Black. Again their perceptions and attitudes are not congruent. Factors other than knowledge of status must also be relevant during the adolescent period, factors such as self-identification and peer relations.

CONTACT IN A MULTI-ETHNIC SCHOOL

Although many children continue to live in ethnically homogeneous neighbourhoods, a number of them attend mixed schools. People generally assume that contact with another ethnic group reduces prejudice because familiarity reduces threat and enhances knowledge of what the two have in common. Evidence for the contact hypothesis, as this is called, has been mixed (see Hewstone and Brown, 1986). Consequently, the goal of research has been to specify the narrow conditions under which contact reduces prejudice, such as equal status interaction. One major limitation of this research is that contact may not actually be responsible for the reduction; some other psychological process coinciding or overlapping with contact seems to be the critical factor. Thus, studies which examine prejudice in relation to proportion of each group in the community or to interpersonal contact per se are missing the key variable (Hewstone and Brown, 1986). In the child literature it has also become apparent that because of resegregation (Schofield, 1986), proportions of each ethnic group in the school do not tell the whole story. Researchers are beginning to look at other factors such as an unbiased school structure or interpersonal friendship. A second major limitation of the contact research is that a positive attitude toward the contacted outgroup member does not often generalize to other members. This, according to Hewstone and Brown, is due to the emphasis on interpersonal rather than intergroup contact. The research on children also emphasizes individual contact and friendship because these are relatively easy for children to initiate and sustain on their own. However, one could also generate occasions for intergroup contact in a school setting.

Given that most school studies distinguish between high and low contact schools in terms of proportions, I will initially use this variable to discuss the research. To be accurate, the results are probably the effects of exposure and whatever that entails rather than the effects of contact. Each of the three theories identifies what is important about exposure and what the effect should be on prejudice. Attending a multi-ethnic school could, on the one hand, make children more aware of the status differences between groups. According to the social reflection theory, this would enhance prejudice. On the other hand, if the ratio is close to 50:50 children would also have the opportunity to become acquainted with individual children from the other ethnic group. Becoming familiar with the qualities of an individual would reduce the salience of group status differences. According to the inner-state authoritarian theory of prejudice, children will not displace or project negative qualities on to people whom they know. According to the cognitive developmental theory, at 8 years of age children begin to develop capabilities that allow them to understand individual qualities and to form personal friendships. Given the opportunity, they will cease to focus on group divisions and instead focus on individual qualities and differences. In summary, the social reflection theory would predict higher prejudice toward minority groups in all children attending multi-ethnic schools; whereas the inner-state and cognitive developmental theories would predict lower prejudice in multi-ethnic compared to mono-ethnic schools.

Most studies do find a difference in prejudice between these two types of schools in that there is less prejudice toward minorities in multi-ethnic schools. White children express more liking for the Black, Asian or Native Indian child when the ratio is close to 50:50 than when it is close to 90:10 (Davey, 1983; Fox and Jordan, 1973; Friedman, 1980; George and Hoppe, 1979; Goldstein et al., 1979; Rohrer, 1977). When the samples include children under 8 years, the data for these younger children are less consistent. For example, Milner (1973) found no school differences with 5- to 8-year-old children, and neither did Brown and Johnson (1971) with 3- to 6-year-olds. The evidence presented here suggests that many White children show less prejudice when they attend multi-ethnic schools, particularly when they are older. However, it should also be pointed out that in an earlier review of the literature, Stephan (1978) concluded that White prejudice either was the same in the two types of schools or was higher in multi-ethnic schools when the children were lower SES. Perhaps the Black children in these schools simply confirmed the Whites' perception of the status differential. In addition, the parental hostility generated by early attempts at desegregation may have prevented children from getting to know members of the other group at an individual level and have condoned prejudice.

Black children attending multi-ethnic schools appear to show less White preference and more Black preference than Blacks attending predominantly Black schools (Goldstein et al, 1979; Rohrer, 1977). However, in two other studies, there were no school differences (Fox and Jordan, 1973; Milner, 1973). Among older Blacks who often show prejudice toward Whites, Stephan (1978) concluded that multi-ethnic schools produced a reduction in White prejudice, especially when the

Black children developed friendships with the White children. Thus, in the early years, contact with Whites at school seems to facilitate Blacks' liking for their own group, whereas in the later years it helps to reduce prejudice toward Whites.

School exposure to Whites can have another effect on young minority children. Werner and Idella (1968) assessed the ethnic categorization and preferences of 4- and 5-year-old Hispanic children who either attended or did not attend a preschool. Those who attended the preschool showed more ethnic categorization and more White preference than did those who did not attend preschool. These authors concluded that the exposure to White teachers and White education values influenced the children to adopt pro-White attitudes. The children were probably too young to become aware of the status differential in the society at large. However, they may have become aware of the status differences in their classroom, between teachers who were White and children. They then may have generalized teacher status to White people in general. In contrast, those who did not attend the preschool and who lived in a homogeneous neighbourhood preferred their own group. This study raises an interesting question about how young children conceptualize status differences between ethnic groups. If asked who most people would think best, probably the children in and out of preschool would say that most people would think Hispanics best. Indeed, most of the people they know would think Hispanics best because most of the people they know are Hispanics. If asked who 'important' people would think best, the preschool children would probably say that White teachers are important people because they control the resources of the school, and they think Whites are best. By this hypothetical example, I am suggesting that young children may conceptualize status in terms of whom 'important' people think are best. Important people may be those whom the children think receive and control desired resources such as toys and books. Davey (1983) was probably tapping the same idea by asking children who they would most like to be. Although the Blacks and Asians knew who they were, over half of the children from 7 to 10 years said they would most like to be White. This answer seems to reflect their awareness of who has the highest status in the society. The children's answer to this question was also related to their preferences. The number of children wanting to be White declined with age parallel with preferences.

This review of the evidence indicates that the effect of exposure to another ethnic group is not strong in itself. Some White children attending a multi-ethnic school where the ratio approximates 50:50 may be less prejudiced than those who attend a predominantly White school, particularly those older than 8 years. The effect of exposure to Whites on Black children depends on their age. In the early years, exposure to Whites may serve to make them pro-White; later exposure facilitates a more positive attitude toward Blacks, and later still a more positive attitude toward Whites. Again, the findings are not strong though the trend is in this direction. Some researchers have suggested that the results are not strong because exposure in itself does not reduce prejudice. The exposure is effective only if it brings about different types of contact such as interpersonal contact and intergroup contact (Pettigrew, 1986), the former to enhance within-group differentiation and the latter to enhance between-group differentiation (see chapter 7).

That exposure itself is not effective has been made clear in both experimental and field observation studies. Katz and Zalk (1978) asked 8- and 11-year-old White children to work with others on a puzzle. Some groups consisted of four White children and some consisted of two Whites working with two Black children. Although there were incentives to work together, the White children did not interact very much with the Blacks. In a posttest of their attitudes, those who had worked with the Blacks showed no less prejudice than those who had worked with other Whites. Exposure in this case was very short-term; there was probably neither intergroup nor interpersonal contact. Reports of social behaviour in multi-ethnic schools clearly demonstrate that exposure by itself does not produce interaction. Same-ethnic interactions and same-ethnic ratings of liking exceed cross-ethnic ones for both Black and White elementary school children (St John and Lewis, 1975; Schofield and Francis, 1982; Singleton and Asher, 1979). This is not to say that children shun cross-ethnic friendships. Using a finer-grained analysis which examined reciprocated liking in dyads, Whitley et al. (1984) found a number of friendships characterized by mutual liking in pairs of cross-ethnic children. That is, even though children may not be generally popular with children from the other ethnic groups, they do form friendships with a few. A few close friendships probably contribute more to one's development than does general popularity with one's classmates.

The problem with these descriptions of cross-ethnic friendship is that they may take place only among children who already possess positive attitudes toward the other group. In this case, friendship is a consequence rather than a cause of positive attitudes. To examine whether friendship changes one's attitudes, we would ideally put children, regardless of their prior attitudes, into contact with children from another ethnic group and tell them to become friends. We all know, however, that forced friendships do not work. Short of this, educators have designed intervention programmes to help children become acquainted with the qualities and accomplishments of minority groups. This type of intervention may serve to enhance within-group and/or between-group differentiation, just as contact does, but without any contact. Generally, these programmes seem to be effective in reducing prejudice (e.g. Bunton and Weissbach, 1974; Crooks, 1970; Likover, 1971). White children between 4 and 7 years participating in these programmes become more favourable toward Blacks. Likewise, Black children express more preference for Blacks and more Black self-identification than children who are not enrolled. Once again it should be noted that the effects of this exposure are not strong. The White children did not become pro-Black but simply less prejudiced toward Blacks.

Katz (1973) developed two other strategies for facilitating familiarity with individuals from different ethnic groups. One strategy is called distinctive labelling training. The Black and White children were shown faces of other Black and White children and asked to learn the names of each over many trials. This forced the children to attend to individual features of children from the other group in order to learn their individual names. They had to overcome their tendency to categorize the children as Black and attend only to their group features. A second strategy is called perceptual differentiation training. The children in this condition were shown pairs of faces of outgroup children. They were required to make a judgement about each pair indicating how similar or different they were to each other. Initially the children saw the faces as similar, but gradually they began to notice individual differences. White children who were trained in these two ways to attend to individual rather than only group features became less prejudiced toward Blacks; and Blacks became less prejudiced toward Whites. Compared to a group of children who simply looked at the faces with no encouragement to attend to individual features, the trained children showed more favourable attitudes. These strategies were more effective in reducing prejudice with 12-year-olds than with 7-year-olds, perhaps because older children were more cognitively capable of attending to individual features and individual personalities. Because older children are able to think about internal personal qualities in addition to concrete facial features, they may have imagined distinct personalities that went along with these faces. A fact often overlooked is that social interventions work best when they are geared to the cognitive capabilities of the child. More will be said about this in chapter 7 when cognitive factors that contribute to reducing prejudice are discussed.

EXAMINERS' ETHNICITY

Some researchers have found that children are less prejudiced when tested by a person from the group toward which they would otherwise be prejudiced. In other words, when compared with children who were tested by a person from their preferred group, these children show less prejudice. Such findings are more often reported for White than for minority children, especially when the children are 7 years or older (e.g. Clark et al., 1980; Katz, 1973; Katz et al., 1975). On occasion they have been found with younger White children (e.g. Corenblum and Wilson, 1982; Katz and Zalk, 1974; Williams and Morland, 1976), and with minority children (e.g. Katz, 1973; Katz et al., 1975; Katz and Zalk, 1974). The evidence from a larger number of studies, however, indicates that the examiner's ethnicity has no effect on children's attitudes (Banks and Rompff, 1973; Bunton and Weissbach, 1974; Corenblum and Wilson, 1982; Friedman, 1980; Goldstein et al., 1979; Katz et al., 1975; Moore, 1976; Williams and Morland, 1976).

Overall, then, the evidence is largely though not entirely in the direction of showing little effect of examiner's ethnicity. However, because the examiner does appear to have an effect on some children, it is worth understanding what the effect might be. Although it is found more frequently with White children, minority children are sometimes similarly affected by the examiner. Likewise, it is not specific to certain tests of prejudice and therefore is not simply a criticism of a measure. Several explanations have been offered. Upon examining them, it becomes clear why the phenomenon is not widespread. The explanations are applicable to certain individuals but not to others, or to certain age groups but not to others. Perhaps the narrow scope of the explanations accounts for why some but not all children are affected by their examiner's ethnicity.

One explanation concerns the child's need for approval and the desire to obtain approval from the examiner. Recall that the need for approval is higher in some children than in others. It is usually measured by the Children's Social Desirability Scale developed by Crandall, Crandall and Katkovsky (1965) on which children show a range of scores. One way to obtain approval is to say that you like the examiner and like people from the examiner's ethnic group. This explanation might account for the answers given by a young child, because it is a very egocentric and socially unsophisticated way of obtaining approval. Another way to obtain approval is to present yourself as unprejudiced knowing that this is a socially desirable quality. This is a socially more sophisticated way of obtaining approval because it requires that one understands the undesirability of prejudice. Thus, it might account for the answers given by some older children. The approval explanation, however, can only account for the answers given by children who have a high need for approval. Because the need for approval declines with age, we would expect it to influence younger more than older children.

A second explanation rests on the idea that certain events prime related cognitions that exist in the child. A child may know at one level that Blacks are as good as Whites, but that knowledge may remain inactive or forgotten until some event triggers it. Being tested by a Black examiner may make that knowledge salient because it reminds the child that Black persons hold important positions. Thus, the event of being tested by a Black examiner primes the child's cognition that Blacks can be good and friendly. This explanation clearly is relevant only if the child has a latent cognition that people from that ethnic group are good. If no cognition exists, then there is nothing to be primed. If the cognition is strong and active, then no event is needed to prime it; it would be salient whenever ethnic issues are discussed. There is some evidence that such cognitions develop during the years from 6 to 12. With age, children are more likely to say that both own and other group members can be good, and to say that respect and fairness are important (Davey, 1983; Davidson, 1976; Doyle et al., 1987). The priming explanation, therefore, accounts for the fact that very young children and older 12-year-olds are less affected than those in middle childhood by the examiner's race (Clark et al., 1980; Katz, 1973; Katz et al., 1975). The priming explanation also shows why the examiner's ethnicity sometimes has other effects on children such as making them more rather than less prejudiced. In Katz's (1973) control group of highly prejudiced 7-year-old children, the Black examiner elicited more prejudiced responses than the White examiner. Presumably, the children possessed cognitions that Blacks were bad and unfriendly, cognitions which were made more salient by the Black examiner. The priming effect may also explain why young Native Indian children identified more strongly with Indians when tested by an Indian examiner, though their preference for Whites did not differ as a function of the examiner (Corenblum and Annis, 1987). Here one would have to assume that the Native Indian children possessed latent cognitions that they were Indian but no cognition that Indians were preferable. Given the findings reported in chapters 3 and 4, this is quite a reasonable assumption.

At this point, it is not clear which of these two explanations is the correct one. More likely, each explains a certain subset of children who are affected by the examiner's ethnicity. The need for approval accounts particularly well for the less prejudiced responses given by young White children when tested by a Black examiner. In other circumstances, it would appear that the examiner's ethnicity primes certain prior but weak cognitions. It should be remembered that only some children are affected by the examiner's ethnicity. This fact lends credibility to the two explanations because both are specific to certain individuals and more relevant to certain age groups. One might question why I have taken the space to develop explanations of a finding that is inconsistent. Despite its inconsistency, the finding that some children react to the examiner's ethnicity is not a phantom. Rather than simply blaming the tests for allowing children to hide their prejudice, we might gain an understanding about cross-ethnic interaction by looking at the dynamics of the testing situation. The explanations suggest that factors related to the child's inner state as well as to the interpersonal event are important in this situation. It is precisely because children vary so much in their inner needs and cognitions that the effect is so sporadic. If it were an effect of the examiner's ethnicity only, then it would be more consistent.

However, it is clear that the cross-ethnic situation is not the usual place for discussing one's prejudices. It may be an interesting interaction to study but it complicates the assessment of attitudes. To measure attitudes, one would simplify matters by using an examiner from the child's own or family ethnic group because these are the people to whom children usually express their feelings.

PARENTAL ETHNOCENTRISM AND AUTHORITARIANISM

Perhaps the most widely held belief about the formation of ethnic attitudes is that children adopt their parents' attitudes. One version of the social reflection theory, that described by Allport (1954), claims that children learn prejudice from their parents. They learn either by direct instruction, as when a parent tells a child not to play with outgroup children because they are not nice, or by observing the parents' words or actions toward people from the outgroup. Allport believed that children imitated their parents' emotional reactions to others because children identify with their parents and because children want to please their parents. This explanation rings true, given what we know about the influence of parents on their children. Children do indeed imitate many things that their parents say and do. The question is, do they also adopt their parents' attitudes.

The evidence suggests that children do not always adopt their parents' ethnic attitudes, and if they do it is usually after 7 years of age. This conclusion comes from research where both parents and children have been given tests measuring their attitudes toward their own and other ethnic groups. The parents' scores are then correlated with the child's score to determine whether parents who are prejudiced have prejudiced children. One large study found no such relation between the scores of parents and their children. Davey (1983) found that though White children between 7 and 10 years were prejudiced toward Blacks and Asians, their parents were quite accepting of these two groups. Similarly, there was no systematic relation between the attitudes of Black and Asian children and those of their parents. One study did find a relation between the ethnocentrism of 6- and 7-year-old White children and their mothers (Mosher and Scodel, 1960). The correlation coefficient was 0.32. Children of highly ethnocentric mothers held more negative attitudes toward 10 ethnic groups using a Social Distance measure than did children of less ethnocentric mothers.

Children seem to think that their parents hold attitudes similar to their own. In one study by Epstein and Komorita (1966), White children between 9 and 11 years were asked to fill in one ethnocentrism scale for themselves and one for their parents. Their ratings on the two scales were significantly correlated ($r = 0.48$). It would seem that the children are strong supporters of Allport's theory of prejudice. However, because the relation was found between children's reports of their parents' ethnocentrism and not the parents' actual ethnocentrism, a simpler explanation is plausible. The children may simply believe that their attitudes are correct and that their parents also see the world the way they do.

The influence of parents is particularly weak when their children are young. Branch and Newcombe (1980) found that Black parents who were active in promoting Black rights had children who were pro-White; in fact they were more pro-White than were children whose parents were not active. In a subsequent study, these same authors conducted more extensive testing of Black parents' ethnic attitudes and attitudes toward teaching their children about racial matters. The parents' attitudes were inversely related to the attitudes of their 4- and 5-year-old children ($r = -0.56$ and -0.60). Parents who were pro-Black and who taught their children pro-Black attitudes had pro-White children. This evidence strongly contradicts the theory that young children adopt the attitudes taught or held by their parents.

Older Black children seem to hold attitudes more in line with their parents'. Although not consistently related, parent and child attitudes are at least positively rather inversely correlated. Branch and Newcombe (1986) gave the same tests to parents of 6- and 7-year-olds and found that the correlations were positive though only one in four was significant. The authors point out that parents' teachings did have an effect on the child's knowledge and awareness of racial matters at both ages. However, in the early years, children may derive from this knowledge only the idea that Whites are superior to Blacks. They extract from their parents' teachings what is meaningful to them. Initially, they are attentive to information about who controls and possesses important resources such as toys (Bandura, Ross and Ross, 1963; Gottfried and Gottfried, 1974). They imitate and prefer people who have this kind of power. Thus, for a young child, status is very meaningful and group affiliation is not. As they grow older, children may extract from their parents' teachings an awareness of how group affiliation is tied to personal preferences.

The parent–child correlations obtained by Spencer (1983) may lead to the same conclusion although no analyses were conducted on the separate age groups. Spencer gave the Preschool Racial Attitude Measure to Black children from 3 to 9 years of age. She divided the scale into two scores, one reflecting personal preference (e.g. Which one would you like as a playmate?) and one reflecting social values (e.g. Everyone says how ugly one boy is. Which one is ugly?). With age, the children showed a tendency to become less pro-White and more pro-Black. Their mothers were given a questionnaire asking them about their strategies for teaching racial matters. The children's social values were more pro-Black if their mothers taught them about civil rights and discussed racial discrimination. The children were more pro-White if their mothers knew a lot about Black history and felt positively toward the current racial climate and toward integration. Thus, social values held by the children were affected by their mothers' discussion of Black experiences in a White society. This specific instruction resulted in the children being more pro-Black, but this attitude was not very apparent until the children were 7 years old. Thus, the results are similar to those reported by Branch and Newcombe (1986) in that parental attitudes and strategies for discussing racial matters do not begin to be reflected in the attitudes of Black children until after the age of 6 or 7.

The preceding discussion revolved around the idea that children learn their ethnic preferences from their parents. There are other reasons why prejudiced parents may have prejudiced children. The authoritarian theory of prejudice states that prejudiced parents have a certain style of child-rearing which arouses but does not allow for the controlled expression of hostility in their children. The children feel anxious about admitting that they are angry toward their parents, so instead they direct their anger toward minority groups. This theory has found some support when applied to White parents and their children.

First, there is evidence that prejudiced parents have different ways of thinking about themselves as parents and of relating to their children. Mosher and Scodel (1960) found that parents who scored high on an ethnocentrism scale of prejudice also used authoritarian child-rearing practices. That is, prejudiced parents tended to use more punitive strategies, to punish hostility in their children and to base their power on their status as parents. For these parents, status and power justified that they be dominant and that they demand submission from their children. In contrast, nonauthoritarian practices emphasized the individual needs of children and parents more than their status. Rather than simply punishing the inevitable anger that children express toward their parents, they attempted to understand the anger and help the child to express it in socially acceptable ways.

Further, Mosher and Scodel found that the attitudes held by 6- and 7-year-old White children were related to the ethnocentrism and the authoritarian practices of their parents. That is, parents who were ethnocentric and parents who used authoritarian practices tended to have more prejudiced children. However, of these two parental qualities ethnocentrism was the stronger determinant of children's attitudes. Parents who were ethnocentric regardless of their child-rearing practices produced prejudiced children. Parents who were authoritarian did not have children who were more prejudiced unless the parents were also ethnocentric. Epstein and Komorita (1966) support these results with children aged 9 to 11 years. This suggests that parents' punitiveness toward their children has little effect by itself. The unresolved hostility it arouses in children has little effect on their attitudes unless the punitive parent is also ethnocentric. A punitive parent may arouse hostility, but this hostility is not directed toward minority groups unless the parent indicates that such groups are appropriate targets for hostility. This explanation of prejudice rests on two processes that may converge in some children 7 years of age and older. One is the development of an inner state characterized by unresolved hostility and due to certain authoritarian child-rearing practices. The other is a learning process whereby children learn from their parents that certain people are not good and are therefore appropriate targets of anger.

Another aspect of the authoritarian theory of prejudice is that punitive child-rearing practices instil a low self-esteem in children. Parents who frequently punish their child's anger and other impulses are essentially conveying the message that the child is bad. The child eventually internalizes this message in the form of a low self-evaluation. The theory goes on to assert that in order to avoid carrying all the blame themselves, children project or generalize their negative qualities onto other people.

The people they choose to derogate are those whom their parents and others derogate. This aspect of the theory has been supported by Bagley's research with young adolescents (Bagley, Mallick and Verma, 1979; Bagley, Verma, Mallick and Young, 1979). Prejudice was found to be higher in adolescents with low self-esteem than in those with high self-esteem. Moreover, those with low self-esteem tended to have authoritarian fathers. Bagley claims, then, that authoritarian fathers produce low self-esteem in their children, particularly their sons, and that it is the low self-esteem rather than attitude learning per se that leads to prejudice. In addition to having low self-esteem, prejudiced adolescents tend to have prejudiced fathers and prejudiced friends. Once again, we see that two factors converge in the highly prejudiced person. One is an inner state of feeling negative about oneself, and the other is a social network that approves of prejudice.

Although Bagley claimed to trace the adolescents' low self-esteem to their fathers' authoritarian child-rearing practices, there are other explanations for their low self-esteem. Prejudiced adolescents also tended to have lower IQs and to be rejected by their peers more than unprejudiced adolescents. These two qualities are very strongly associated with low self-esteem. Thus, the children's own school and peer experiences rather than their father's authoritarian style could account for their negative feelings about themselves.

In summary, this section examined various parent factors that have been associated with prejudice in children. Parents' ethnocentrism is often but not always associated with higher prejudice in children, particularly children older than 7 years. It would seem then that the children must reach a certain level of development before they understand and internalize their parents' attitudes. They do not simply imitate adult attitudes in total. They adopt only what fits their needs or their way of thinking. Thus, a learning theory of prejudice must take into account what the child brings to the situation, and not simply what the parent tells the child. With respect to parents' authoritarianism, it appears that child-rearing practices do not by themselves produce prejudice in children. Although no definitive conclusions can be made at this point, the little evidence that does exist suggests that an authoritarian upbringing leads to prejudice by making the child more dependent on ethnocentric parents and possibly by lowering the child's self-esteem.

SELF-ESTEEM

A great deal of controversy surrounds the idea that ethnic attitudes are related to self-esteem. In White children the relation is understood simply as a consequence of ethnocentric and authoritarian parenting. According to Bagley, Mallick and Verma (1979), low self-esteem leads to a strong preference for one's own group and a strong dislike of minority groups. The explanation is based on the psychodynamic principle that negative self-esteem is uncomfortable and so is transformed into a negative esteem for minority groups and an exaggerated positive esteem for one's own group. A similar explanation offered by Tajfel's (1978) and Turner's (1978) group self-enhancement theory is that majority group members with low self-esteem try to enhance themselves through association with their high-status group because they do not feel competent to do it through their own activities. In either case, the low self-esteem person attempts to obtain higher esteem by perceiving his/ her own group as superior and other groups as inferior. There is also the suggestion of a drive underlying this perception; because people feel uncomfortable with low self-esteem, they will adamantly argue for something that raises their self-esteem.

Interestingly, the opposite relation between prejudice and esteem has been assumed for Black children. It has been taken for granted that Black children have low self-esteem when they indicate a preference for Whites over Blacks. In other words, the assumption is that when Blacks prefer another group to their own, they also have low self-esteem. The controversy arose over whether attitudes toward one's own group directly reflected the attitudes one held about oneself, that is, whether 'ingroup hatred' reflected 'self-hatred'. Subsequent studies on the self-esteem of White, Black and Hispanic children indicated that self-esteem was equally high among Blacks and Whites but lower among Hispanic children (Fu, Hinkle and Korslund, 1983; Rosenberg and Simmons, 1971; Stephan and Rosenfield, 1979). There is no evidence of widespread self-hatred among Blacks in the United States though other minority children may have somewhat lower self-esteem (e.g. Lefley, 1975). In one study, the lower esteem of Hispanic children was accounted for by their lower school achievement and their father's education (Stephan and Rosenfield, 1979).

A question of greater importance is whether self-esteem is related to ethnic attitudes within individuals. The work of Bagley discussed previously indicated that the two are related in White adolescents. Those with lower self-esteem were more prejudiced than those with higher self-esteem. Among younger White children there seems to be no relation between self-esteem and prejudice (Katz et al., 1975; Stephan and Rosenfield, 1979), regardless of whether self-esteem is measured by the real–ideal discrepancy or by standardized tests such as the one used by Bagley. Their self-esteem is strongly related to their social class, to having both parents present and to school achievement (Rosenberg and Simmons, 1971; Stephan and Rosenfield, 1979), but not to ethnic attitudes. Thus, White children seem to derive and maintain their self-esteem through comparisons with their own group on performance and social status, and not by disliking a minority group.

Tajfel's (1978) theory proposes that when ethnic divisions are salient, White children will compare themselves with other ethnic groups in order to enhance their worth. However, such interethnic comparisons do not seem to be made by children. Aboud (1976) gave White children from a multi-ethnic school the opportunity to compare themselves with White and Hispanic children who performed better or worse. Tajfel's theory would predict that they would compare themselves with Whites who performed better and Hispanics who performed worse. They did not. They consistently compared themselves with Whites regardless of performance. Thus, spontaneous comparisons were made with own-group members only.

Among Black children, there is an inconsistent relation between self-esteem and prejudice. In two studies, no relation was found between self-esteem and attitudes toward Blacks and Whites (Katz et al., 1975; Spencer, 1982). However, the children in two other studies were more positive toward their own group and less positive toward Hispanics and Whites if they had high self-esteem (Stephan and Rosenfield, 1979; Ward and Braun, 1972). Overall, the children in these two studies were very positive toward Blacks, so even those with low self-esteem were probably not negative but rather neutral toward their own group. Thus, there is very little evidence for the idea that low esteem for Blacks reflects low esteem for oneself. There is some evidence that Blacks with high self-esteem are more positive toward Blacks and more negative toward others.

The self-esteem of Native Indian children was found in one study to be related to both own-group preference and to own-group identification (George and Hoppe, 1979). The relation was found for 8- and 10-year-old Indians but not for 12-year-olds. Overall, these children preferred and identified with Whites, though children who held a positive attitude toward themselves showed more attachment toward their own group over Whites. Also, unlike other studies, this one measured positive self-esteem in terms of spontaneously mentioned positive descriptors of oneself rather than responses to a standardized test of self-esteem.

No relation between self-esteem and attitudes has been found with Hispanic children in the one study that examined it (Stephan and Rosenfield, 1979). However, there is evidence that Hispanic children evaluate themselves on the basis of their school achievement (Stephan and Rosenfield, 1979), and in a multi-ethnic school compare themselves with Whites as well as with other Hispanics. Aboud (1976) gave Hispanic children the opportunity to compare their performance with Hispanics and Whites who performed better or worse. The children were evenly divided in their interethnic comparison strategies. Some consistently compared with Hispanics, some consistently with Whites, and some with a Hispanic who performed better and with a White who performed worse. Only the last group were making biased comparisons that would favour their ethnic group; the others were consistently choosing one ethnicity as their reference group. These findings address the question of whether multi-ethnic schools provide the opportunity for interethnic comparisons that lower self-esteem and the perceived status of minority groups. They suggest that only one-third of the children make interethnic comparisons that put them and their group at a disadvantage. Most of the children seem to use their own ethnic ingroup as a comparison group or make contrasts that favour their own group.

NEED FOR APPROVAL

The need for approval may be seen as an aspect of self-esteem. Although those with a high need for approval do not necessarily possess a low self-esteem, they may have a greater need for self-enhancement. The need for approval is measured by a scale that determines whether respondents describe themselves excessively in terms of socially desirable qualities (Crowne and Marlowe, 1964). The authors assumed that people expect to obtain approval from others if they appear in socially desirable ways, such as always being good, kind and happy. By denying that they possess any negative or undesirable qualities, people hope to avoid disapproval. Thus, people who present themselves unrealistically as possessing mostly desirable qualities reveal a high need for approval or fear of disapproval.

The need for approval may be related to prejudice in two ways. Firstly, by identifying with and preferring higher status Whites, children may be seeking to adopt a desirable attitude and thereby gain approval. Secondly, children may assume that Whites are given more approval by authority figures, and that by associating with Whites they too will gain approval.

Using the Social Desirability Scale for children, researchers have found that girls have a higher need for approval than boys, that Black children have a higher need for approval than Whites and that need for approval declines with age (Crandall et al., 1965). It was also found that younger White children attribute more prejudice to their examiner than do older children (Doyle et al., 1987). Thus, younger children may be more prejudiced than older ones because they assume that authority figures value certain groups over others and will give approval to children who likewise hold these values. The high need for approval combined with the cognition that approval will be given for preferring Whites could account for higher pro-White attitudes among younger children, both White and minority. It could also account for the decline in pro-White attitudes with age as children's need for approval declines and other needs dominate. Because girls generally have a higher need for approval than boys, especially in the early years, one might expect young girls to be more pro-White. There is some evidence for this sex difference, though it is generally not the case.

In addition to wanting adult approval of themselves, young children seem to prefer others who obtain adult approval. This was demonstrated in two studies. In one, the 4- and 5-year-old White children viewed puppets who either handed out rewards to others, received these rewards or were ignored. The children preferred the puppet who received rewards over the other two (Gottfried and Gottfried, 1974). Although children often imitate the person who controls the rewards, they prefer the person who obtains the rewards. To the extent that children equate concrete rewards with adult approval, their preferences appear to be strongly influenced by adult approval. This conclusion alerts us to the possibility that children perceive status in two ways. Status may be derived from controlling resources as adults do (Bandura et al., 1963), and status may also come from receiving desired resources and approval. The latter seems to be more important in determining children's preferences for some children over others.

In a second study, children of 6 and 7 years were shown photos of Black and White children. Both Black and White children preferred the White photo over the Black one. They were then read stories about pairs of these children. In one story the White received adult approval and the Black received disapproval. In another story the Black received adult approval and the White received disapproval. Overall, the children's preferences were strongly influenced by the approval information. White children were equally divided into those who based their preferences on skin colour alone and those who based their preferences on adult approval. More of the Black children based their preferences on approval than on skin colour, that is, they preferred the White who gained approval in the first story and the Black who gained approval in the second story. One might infer that their initial preference for Whites was based on the assumption that Whites generally gain more approval than Blacks.

Although the need for approval is usually regarded as an individual difference variable and a dimension of personality, it is possible to view it as a developmental variable that declines with age. Thus, although certain children are more or less in need of approval compared to their own age group, all children seem to need less approval as they grow older. This need may be tied to cognitive development. As such it may explain the decline in prejudice with age.

SEX DIFFERENCES IN PREJUDICE

In an earlier review of studies on ethnic attitudes, Brand et al. (1974) concluded that girls are more influenced by White social norms than boys, and that girls from different ethnic groups prefer Whites more than boys. This sex difference has not been upheld in recent research. In one study, only Asian girls were more pro-White than boys, whereas White and Black girls were less pro-White (Fox and Jordan, 1973). None of these differences was great. Likewise, in another study, Black girls showed less preference for Whites than boys (Asher and Allen, 1969). Contradictory results from other studies indicate that both White and Black girls are more ethnocentric than boys (Goldstein et al., 1979), and that White and Black girls are less intolerant than boys (Katz et al., 1975). Only one study confirmed that minority girls are more interested in White norms than boys. Native Indian and Chinese Asian girls chose to look at more White picture books and fewer Black or other ethnic books than did boys (Aboud, 1977). However, this interest was not reflected in their attitude ratings.

These reported sex differences are very inconsistent and probably unreliable. Most of the studies reviewed here report no sex differences (Brown and Johnson, 1971; Bunton and Weissbach, 1974; Davey, 1983; Epstein et al., 1976; Fox and Jordan, 1973; Friedman, 1980; Katz et al., 1975; Katz and Zalk, 1974; Milner, 1973; Newman et al., 1983; Spencer, 1983; Vaughan, 1964; Ward and Braun, 1972; Weiland and Coughlin, 1979; Werner and Idella, 1968; Williams et al., 1975).

SUMMARY OF SOCIAL AND PSYCHOLOGICAL FACTORS

The research on social stratification indicates that ethnic heterogeneity does not itself produce prejudice. There must be a history of ethnic status differences or current status differences in the community. Whether positive attitudes are directed toward the higher status group or toward the ingroup depends on the child's ethnicity and age. White children's preference for Whites could be the result of either factor since they both lead to the same outcome. In minority groups one finds the former more among children under 7 years and the latter more among older children. The effects of stratification on prejudice may depend both on strategies for self-enhancement through approval seeking, and on the level of self-esteem. Both White and minority children with a high need for approval or low self-esteem may be more pro-White than those with a lower need for approval or a high self-esteem. Whites from the latter two groups may also be less negative toward minorities; whereas Blacks and Native Indians from the latter two groups may be more positive toward their own group.

The child's socio-economic status is not strongly related to prejudice. In White children there is no evidence for a relation. In minority children the evidence is mixed but it is possible that SES affects their attitudes differently as a function of their age. There is very little information about how children perceive the status of various ethnic groups and their own. By 8 years of age children seem to perceive status differences, though these are based on concrete attributes other than actual political or economic power. They may be based on who controls or receives rewards such as adult approval. They also depend largely on whether the child is capable of and has the opportunity to make comparisons between ethnic groups. Children under 12 years tend to live in homogeneous environments and to derive their status through comparisons with their own group. Those who function in multi-ethnic environments or those who are capable of making broad social comparisons do not generally translate these comparisons into an evaluation of themselves or their group as inferior or unlikeable.

Exposure in a multi-ethnic school may serve only to enhance the status differential if the ratio is 90:10. However, if the ratio is 50:50, contact with minorities appears to reduce prejudice among White children over 8 years. Among minority children, school contact may have different effects at different ages. Children of 4 and 5 years may become more pro-White with contact; children in the middle childhood years may be more favourable toward their own group as a result of contact; and older children may be less prejudiced toward Whites with contact. These findings are generally less consistent for children under 8 years. Contact probably has an effect on ethnic attitudes only when both interpersonal and intergroup aspects of the interaction are salient.

The examiner's ethnicity sometimes reduces the expression of prejudice in White and Black children. Possibly the high need for approval in young children makes them alter their answers toward the attitudes they assume to be held by the examiner. Older children are probably affected because the examiner's ethnicity primes latent cognitions about the likeability of members from other groups, cognitions which become salient on their own at a later age. Both explanations depend on certain expectations or cognitions being held by the child. Overall, the examiner's ethnicity does not appear to be a strong determinant of children's prejudice; most studies find no effect, and those that do, show inconsistent effects.

White parents' attitudes seem to have no direct relation to their children's attitudes, particularly when the parents are favourable toward minorities. However, parents who are ethnocentric may have prejudiced children. If a relation exists, it is more likely to be apparent when the children are 7 years or older. Black parents who are pro-Black tend to have children who are very aware of racial matters and of their racial identity. However, the 4- and 5-year-old children of such parents tend to be more pro-White; the 7-year-old and over children of such parents tend to be more pro-Black. Thus, only when they are cognitively able to interpret their parents' attitudes fully and accurately, do they begin to hold similar attitudes.

Authoritarian child-rearing practices do not directly enhance prejudice in children. In only one instance is there a relation, namely between the father's authoritarianism and his adolescent son's prejudice. This relation may hold because the father's authoritarian style creates a low self-esteem in his son, or because the son has low self-esteem as a result of low school achievement and low peer popularity.

In most research, the self-esteem of White children has no bearing on their level of prejudice. This relation appears only in adolescent Whites. In most White children, self-esteem seems to be related to school achievement and socio-economic status and not to parental authoritarianism or comparisons with an outgroup. The self-esteem of Black children is also frequently unrelated to their ethnic attitudes. However, some studies have found that Blacks with high self-esteem are more pro-Black. There is very little evidence that Black children who are anti-Black have low self-esteem. Native Indian self-esteem may also be related to pro-

Indian attitudes, but no such relation has been found with Hispanic or Asian children.

The need for approval may account for prejudice in young children. Young children seem to have a greater need for approval than older children; they also seem to expect that their parents and examiners are at least if not more prejudiced than they are. In addition, young children prefer people who receive approval from adults. Minority children may assume that Whites generally receive more approval from adults.

There is little evidence for sex differences in prejudice. Although some studies find a sex difference, these differences are inconsistent. Most studies find none.

EVALUATION OF THE SOCIAL REFLECTION THEORY

In light of the evidence, we can now evaluate the validity of the social reflection theory as an explanation of the development of prejudice. What evidence supports this theory? First, there is evidence that children who live in stratified societies may be more prejudiced. However, even children who live in heterogeneous societies with little current stratification show prejudice in the early years. Also, the evidence indicates that both majority White and minority children prefer Whites, who in the societies under investigation are the dominant ethnic group. This preference is largely restricted to the early years from 4 to 8, although it does continue to a certain extent in subsequent years. The early pervasive preference for Whites supports the idea that social values influence ethnic attitudes; the later preference for one's own group supports the idea that parental values influence the ethnic attitudes of children. Thus, different propositions of the theory apply to different age groups.

If the first proposition is true, that social values influence ethnic attitudes in the early years, then children as young as 4 years should show some sensitivity to the status of Whites and non-Whites in their society. The evidence that children under 12 years are sensitive to political and economic status is not strong. However, they may be aware of the differential resources of different ethnic groups, or they may be aware of the differential approval given to different ethnic groups. Approval seems to be particularly important to young children, who as a group have a higher need for approval than older children. Thus, the need for approval combined with the perception of differential approval may account for the young child's sensitivity to social values. If the second proposition is true, that parental attitudes influence older children's attitudes, then children over 8 years should possess attitudes similar to their parents. There is only partial evidence for the similarity between parent's and children's attitudes. For children under 7 years, there appears to be no relation, or even an inverse one in some cases. For children over 7 years, there is some similarity if the White or Black parents are ethnocentric or strongly favour their own group. If the parents are not ethnocentric, there is little similarity because the children are more prejudiced than their parents.

The social reflection theory would predict that exposure to other ethnic groups enhances the awareness of status differences and leads to greater preference for Whites. There is evidence that Black children in mixed ethnic schools are more aware of the status differential, but this does not seem to lead to a greater preference for Whites. Thus, the only evidence in support of the relation between contact and White preference comes from 4- and 5-year-old Hispanic children in a mixed ethnic school. It is not clear whether these very young children are more aware of the status differences between Whites and Hispanics, or are aware of the approval and resources given by White teachers to White children. For the most part, school exposure seems to reduce prejudice toward minority groups in both Whites and Blacks over 8 years. The exposure seems to reduce attention to group differences and increase attention to individual differences in children who are cognitively able to deal with the internal qualities of individuals. Minimal contact in schools with a 90:10 ratio or no contact may have the reverse effect, maintaining attention to group differences because there is no experience with individuals.

In summary, there is some (but not full) support for the social reflection theory's explanation of the development of prejudice. One major weakness is that it cannot explain the shift from social values to parental attitudes as the critical determinant of children's attitudes. The shift occurs around 7 and 8 years of age. A second major weakness is that it cannot explain what aspect of social status is understood by children from 4 to 7 years. A third weakness is in explaining the effects of exposure on the child's awareness of social status, and in explaining why children under 8 years are not affected by exposure. In order to overcome these weaknesses, the theory must incorporate developmental factors that differentiate the child of 7 years and under from the child over 7 years. Certain cognitive developments around 7 and 8 years allow children to identify more strongly with their ethnic group and their parents. These cognitive developments also allow the child to attend to the individual qualities of other people rather than simply to their group qualities.

EVALUATION OF THE INNER STATE AUTHORITARIAN THEORY

The basic proposition of this theory is that authoritarian child-rearing practices of parents determine prejudice in children. There is no evidence for such a relation in the research reported here, except in adolescent boys. There is somewhat more support for the variables thought to mediate this relation, such as self-esteem and need for approval. The high need for approval in young children may make them sensitive to the dominant values in the society or to the values of their examiner. Thus approval from authority may be a concern of young children, though the need for approval itself may not be enhanced by a parent's authoritarianism. The relevant factors here seem to be young children's need for approval and their conformity to authority figures. Self-esteem is not strongly related to prejudice in children under 12 years, though it may mediate the relation between a father's authoritarianism and his adolescent son's prejudice. Finally, the theory would predict that prejudice results from the projection and displacement of hostility on to unknown and therefore ambiguous minority groups. Contact with minority groups would make them less ambiguous and therefore less likely targets of projection and displacement. This aspect of the theory is strongly supported by the research on contact, particularly in White children over 8 years. Contact with and information about minority groups does reduce prejudice if it allows for knowledge about the personal qualities of minority individuals.

The major weakness of the theory, then, is that no relation has been demonstrated between parental authoritarianism and children's prejudice. Another weakness is that the theory addresses individual differences in prejudice among White children; it cannot account for the uniformly high prejudice found among 4- to 7-year-old White children or for the ethnic attitudes of minority group children. However, some of the mediating psychological variables, such as need for approval and lack of knowledge about minority groups, may be related to prejudice. Others such as repressed hostility toward authority and self-esteem are not strongly related to prejudice in children under 12 years.

7 Social-Cognitive Developments Related to Prejudice

The weakness of the social reflection theory and the authoritarian theory resides mainly in their inability to account for age-related changes in prejudice. In particular, the age of 7 appears to be critical for shifts in ethnic attitudes and the factors that determined them. After 7 years of age, White children often show a decline in prejudice and minority children show a more widespread preference for their own group. Also after 7 years of age, children's attitudes are more influenced by various social factors such as their parents' attitudes and the ethnic mix in their school than they are at earlier ages.

This shift around 7 years corresponds to a major shift in cognitive development. Cognitions about the physical world and the social world begin to change at this age and to show many changes over the next five years. Inevitably these cognitive developments affect the way children interpret ethnic differences and their own ethnic affiliation. The way these cognitive developments affect the child's view of ethnicity will be the first topic discussed in this chapter.

The second topic will be the formulation of a social-cognitive developmental theory of prejudice which explains the development of ethnic attitudes in terms of cognitive developments. Cognitive developments taking place after 7 years affect not only how children evaluate members of ethnic groups but also how sensitive they are to social factors in their environment. In a sense, these developments allow children to use more fully the social information provided by their immediate environment – their school, parents and peers.

The theory must also be able to explain the nature of prejudice in children younger than 7 years. This is more difficult because traditional cognitive developmental theory emphasizes the lack of mature cognition rather than the dominance of another process. My view is that the early focus on the self and the early dominance of affective and need states can explain prejudice from 4 to 7 years. Prejudice is therefore initially based on affective processes and then shifts to a cognitive base as cognition dominates the child's functioning. Over the same period, there is a shift in the focus of these processes from being predominantly self-centred to being group and then individual focused. These developments further imply that children will be sensitive only to social factors that address their age-related concerns, initially to self satisfactions and later to group affiliations and to individual affiliations.

COGNITIVE DEVELOPMENTS AFFECTING THE CHILD'S VIEW OF ETHNICITY

Children's understanding of ethnic differences is not surprisingly linked to their understanding of other phenomena, both physical and social. Piaget's theory of cognitive development proposed that children's understanding of social phenomena develop parallel to and are perhaps preceded by their understanding of physical phenomena. This view has been supported by several studies which correlate ethnic cognitions with traditional Piagetian measures of physical cognition. One of the traditional Piagetian measures of cognitive development is the conservation test. Conservation is the ability to understand that quantities of matter remain the same even though they appear to have become larger or smaller. Conservation is often tested by presenting the child with two identical glasses containing the same amount of water. The contents of one are then poured into a differently shaped glass, one that is taller and thinner. The child is asked whether the contents of the two glasses are the same or if one has more. The child who understands conservation will say that the contents are the same, and will explain this by noting that the height of the second glass compensates for its thin width or that no water was removed during the transfer. The child who does not understand conservation will say that the contents are different because one reaches a higher level. The former child's cognitions are able to overcome the misleading perception that the level of water in one glass is higher; the child is able to infer something that is different from what is directly observed.

Another test measuring cognitive development is the test of moral judgement developed by Kohlberg (1976). According to their judgement of moral dilemma stories, children are placed at one of six levels of moral judgement. The early levels are characterized by an emphasis on concrete rewards and satisfactions, the middle levels by an emphasis on conformity to authority, and the later levels by an emphasis on individual judgement.

Children's level of cognitive development as measured by these two tests is related to their understanding of ethnic differences. Three areas of cognitive understanding referred to as ethnic cognitions, are particularly interesting. One is the understanding that members of ethnic groups have psychological as well as concrete attributes. Children at lower developmental levels of Kohlberg's moral judgement scale are more likely to describe members of ethnic groups in terms of concrete appearance or behaviour, whereas those at higher levels use more psychological attributes (Davidson, 1976). A second dimension for assessing an understanding of ethnic differences is in terms of flexibility. Flexibility here refers to the ability to understand that different ethnic groups are not entirely different, that in many respects they are similar, and that individual members of an ethnic group are in many respects different. Conservation correlates highly with having flexible cognitions (Doyle et al., 1987). A third ethnic cognition is ethnic constancy, meaning the understanding that one's ethnicity remains the same despite superficial transformations in skin colour or clothing. Once again, conservation is related to constancy (e.g. Aboud, 1984; Semaj, 1980).

In summary, there is evidence that the way children interpret ethnic differences and ethnic affiliation stems in part from their understanding of other physical and social phenomena. Ethnic cognitions appear to develop as a function of the child's general cognitive development. This is not to say that ethnic cognitions are synonymous with the conservation of physical matter. It is clear that many ethnic cognitions develop after conservation and only when additional knowledge specific to ethnicity has been acquired. However, it does seem to be the case that cognitions about ethnicity develop in relation to cognitions about other phenomena; they are not isolated from the child's general way of thinking about the world.

At this point, it will be useful to elaborate on the three ethnic cognitions in question. In addition to their relation to cognitive development generally, recent research has provided some idea about what these cognitions entail, how they develop with age and how they might in turn affect children's attitudes.

Cognitions about ethnic attributes. What attributes come to mind when a child thinks about a specific ethnic group? I once asked some White children from 6 to 10 years what would have to change for them to become a member of another ethnic group. The attribute varied depending on the ethnic group, but the large majority were external or concrete attributes. To be a Black, they would have to have black skin. The youngest children said this was not possible; whereas the older ones said that they could have black skin if they tanned a long time in the sun, or if someone painted their skin, or if they had been born to Black parents. To be a Native Indian, they would have to speak a different language, or wear Indian clothes with a headdress, or shoot a bow and arrow. Again, the youngest children said that none of these changes were possible; whereas the older ones said they could learn to do these things. This seems to indicate that concrete external attributes are a very salient part of what it means to be White or Black or Indian. In addition, children of 6 or 7 years think of these external ethnic attributes as immutable. Perhaps they did not want to have the other attributes or perhaps they were simply not able to consider two alternatives existing in the same person. Some of the 10-year-olds gave answers that were similar to college students in that they referred to more internal or psychological attributes. For example, older children might say that they would have to change their religious beliefs, or they would have to like different people, or they would have experienced discrimination. These statements indicate not only what attributes distinguish them from others, but also what attributes describe or define a particular ethnic group.

The main conclusion to be drawn from children's descriptions of ethnic groups is that they remain overwhelmingly concerned with external attributes, and therefore with the visible differences between groups (see also Lerner and Buehrig, 1975; Ramsey, 1987). Davidson (1976) designed a game to elicit children's thoughts about various ethnic groups. The game was played on a board with a route mapped out toward becoming an American. When their man landed on a space where a particular ethnic group was pictured, the children were to make a comment about the group. In the excitement of the game, and in their hurry to reach the end goal quickly, the children uninhibitedly generated descriptions. Most of the descriptions given by the elementary school children referred to physical attributes: Italians make good jokes, Irish kids are strong, Indians wear clothes that look like rags, Puerto Ricans are poor, Blacks have guns and start riots. Regardless of whether the attribute is negative or neutral, the comment sounds prejudicial simply because it focuses on a superficial external difference. External attributes, however, are not superficial to a child. They are central to self-identity and they are the basis of friendship. Also, the problem for young children is that their cognitive machinery does not allow for much flexibility, so that on the basis of physical differences they assume that social and psychological attributes are likewise different. Aboud and Skerry (1983) found that the focus on external attributes actually increased from 5 to 9 years of age, whereas the use of internal attributes remained equally low. This was true for one's own ethnic group as well as for other ethnic groups. Furthermore, the increasing use of external attributes for ethnic groups contrasts with its decreasing use in descriptions of the self. Self-descriptions indicate that children of 8 and 9 years are able to think spontaneously about internal qualities; but these more mature thoughts are not applied to ethnic groups until several years later. In this respect, ethnic cognitions are less mature than self-cognitions.

One attribute that children at a young age understand about other ethnic groups is that their preference is for members of their own group. Just as children prefer members of their own group, they likewise assume that other ethnic members will prefer their group. In other words, they are accurate at taking the role of another ethnic person when assigning preferences. However, this breaks down when taking the role of someone from a disliked group (Genesee et al., 1978; Middleton, Tajfel and Johnson, 1970). In the study by Aboud and Mitchell (1977), White children were asked to take the role of a liked, a moderately liked, and a disliked ethnic member and to rate each target child's preference for various ethnic uncles. The children were fairly accurate in assigning an ingroup uncle to their liked and moderately liked peers, but they were inaccurate when it came to the disliked peer. Six-year-olds were inaccurate because they egocentrically thought that such a child would like whomever they liked rather than an uncle from the disliked group. Nine-year-olds were not egocentric; they simply assigned the target a more likeable outgroup uncle to prefer.

One explanation of this breakdown in role taking is that negative attitudes interfere with the full use of one's cognitive capabilities. However, this explanation does not account for the role-taking results obtained from Native Indian children. These children inferred accurate uncle preferences for the disliked target even though they felt as negative toward the group as White children had toward their disliked group. It may be that minority children learn at an earlier age to differentiate attitudes from cognitions. Being able to keep these judgements separate is an important sign of maturity. It allows one to say, 'I do not like this person but I can see that he has good qualities that another might like'; or 'I like this person but I can see that he is not all good'. Minority children may develop the ability earlier because they often experience such a discrepancy in their own ethnic judgements, that is, they may prefer majority White children knowing that they themselves are Native Indian. If not experienced by themselves, they may know others who maintain such an attitude–cognition combination. Few White children would have such an experience. Their ability to differentiate attitudes and cognitions seems to come later.

Whether children can keep attitudes from influencing or dominating their cognitions was examined in another study by Aboud (1981). White children first rated their preferences for five ethnic peers along a continuous scale. They did this by placing stand-up photographs of the peers along a scale of cardboard, closer to themselves the more they liked them and farther away the more they disliked them. The examiner then showed the children a picture of another peer from their disliked group and said that this peer had rated his preferences for the same set of photos. The examiner proceeded to place an identical set of photos on another cardboard scale, indicating that the peer's preferences were the mirror image of the children's. In other words, if a child liked Whites most and Chinese least, then the Chinese peer was said to have liked Chinese most and Whites least; if a child liked Whites most and Blacks least, then the Black peer was said to have liked Blacks most and Whites least. The children were asked to comment on the similarity of the two sets of preferences, their own and their peer's, and all noticed that the two were different. Then they were asked to judge whether both preferences were valid or whether one was wrong or both were wrong. Two-thirds of the children between 5 and 9 years of age thought that only one person's preferences were right and the other was wrong. Some of the children said that only they were right; others said that only the peer was right. Consequently, only 33 per cent understood that two opposite preferences could be equally valid. In my opinion, this understanding demonstrates an ability to separate attitudinal and cognitive judgements. These children understood that a person's preferences could be valid even though he liked someone that the child hated. Predictably, this understanding was more typical of the 8- and 9-year-old children than of the 5- and 6-year-olds. Also, it seems to be related to other social-cognitive measures of differentiation, such as role taking (Weinheimer, 1972). However, it is a mistake to think that simple role taking in terms of inferring the preferences of another ethnic group reduces prejudice. Even prejudiced children can predict that outgroup members prefer their ingroup because this prediction is based on nothing more insightful than social knowledge. The difficult idea to grasp is that an outgroup member's preference is as valid as one's own.

In summary, this section has presented evidence that children develop cognitions about the attributes and preferences of other ethnic groups. These cognitions show a certain immaturity in that they overemphasize external differences, even after the children are able to understand internal self-attributes. Their immaturity is also demonstrated by the fact that they are not strong or salient enough to remain independent of attitudes or affect. Prejudice appears to interfere with children's understanding of ethnic affiliations different from their own. Not until after the age of 8 or 9 are most children knowledgeable about the internal qualities of ethnic members and about the respectability of people one dislikes. These developing cognitions could have the effect of neutralizing strong prejudice. Focusing on internal qualities may reduce the salience of external ethnic differences. Likewise the strengthening of cognitive understanding and the separation of cognition from attitudes may allow cognitions to start influencing attitudes rather than the reverse. Understanding that the people one dislikes are respected and liked by others constitutes a challenge to prejudice that is taken for granted. Interestingly, it was the older children in the Aboud (1981) study who not only acknowledged that both preferences were valid but also subsequently changed their preferences to make them less ethnocentric.

Flexibility in ethnic cognitions.   Flexibility in ethnic cognition refers to the ability to acknowledge two or more different aspects of an ethnic member, aspects which superficially appear to be inconsistent. One index of flexibility is the ability to acknowledge that similar attributes can exist in two individuals who are ethnically different. A second index is the ability to acknowledge that different attributes can exist in two individuals who are ethnically similar. These two forms of flexibility increase with age, particularly around 7 and 8 years and again later in childhood (Davey, 1983; Doyle et al., 1987; Katz et al., 1975). The former (and probably the latter) seem to develop most following the acquisition of conservation. Flexibility, then, is a concrete operational skill that needs as a prerequisite a certain level of cognitive differentiation and inferential ability.

These two forms of flexibility are seen as two sides of the same coin, one emphasizing that children minimize between-group differences and the other that children maximize within-group individual differences. Both are related to prejudice in that less prejudiced children minimize between-group differences and maximize within-group differences more than prejudiced children (Katz et al., 1975). In other words, less prejudiced children have more flexibility in their ethnic cognitions. Flexibility seems to be a cause or determinant of positive attitudes toward other group members. Katz (1973; Katz and Zalk, 1978) trained highly prejudiced children to notice individual differences among children of the ethnic group they disliked. The White children looked at pairs of Black children's faces and the Black children looked at pairs of White children's faces. The children were required either to judge the dissimilarity of the faces or to learn the names of these individuals. This training helped them to maximize their perception of within-group differences. Subsequent tests of prejudice indicated that the children were less prejudiced after the training than they had been before. The training was more effective with 11- and 12-year-olds than with 7- and 8-year-olds, presumably because the older children had the cognitive capability to benefit quickly from the training, that is to develop more flexible cognitions about the other group. In addition, attitudes may be less autonomous and more amenable to the influence of cognitions as children grow older. Perhaps this is what we mean when we say that younger children are more impulsive and older children more reflective. Older children's thoughts are stronger and more salient; older children are more likely to think about things before reacting. Likewise, their thoughts that individual qualities are more important than ethnic qualities may call into question their general negative attitude toward all members of the group.

The technique used by Katz to measure flexibility involved asking children to rate the degree of dissimilarity between pairs of same-ethnic faces and different-ethnic faces. The ratings were made on a 12-point scale where 0 indicated very similar and 11 indicated very dissimilar. A rating of 7 for a Black–White pair and a rating of 2 for a same-ethnic pair would indicate low flexibility. A rating of 3 for a Black–White pair and a rating of 6 or 7 for a same-ethnic pair would indicate high flexibility. Katz found that between 7 and 12 years of age, White children developed greater flexibility in that between-group ratings went down and within-group ratings went up across these years.

Another technique used by Davey (1983) and Doyle et al. (1987) focused exclusively on how between-group differences are perceived. For example, in the Doyle study children were given 20 cards with evaluative descriptions, 10 positive and 10 negative (e.g. smart, wonderful, happy; stupid, selfish, cruel) and asked to put them in the boxes of the people they described. There was a box for each ethnic group as well as a Both box (Davey also used a Nobody box). Davey reported that both Black and White children between the ages of 7 and 10 increasingly used the Both or the Nobody boxes, indicating that they saw fewer differences between Blacks and Whites. Doyle et al. found a similar increase in use of the Both box but noted that the first major jump was before 8 years, between 5 and 8. The second significant jump was between 8 and 12 years. At 5 years of age, most children were assigning the positive descriptions to their own group, the negative descriptions to the other group, and a third of each to the Both box. By 8 years of age, they were assigning over half of the positive and negative descriptions to the Both box, and by 12 years, 80 per cent were assigned to the Both box. The children were expressing flexibility not only because they thought that two different ethnic groups could possess the same qualities, but also because the groups were similar in possessing both positive and negative qualities.

Self-identification and constancy. Identifying one's ethnicity has both perceptual and cognitive components. These processes have already been discussed in chapter 4. However, at this point it might be useful to examine the relation between ethnic identification and ethnic attitudes. With respect to gender identification, Martin and Halverson (1981) propose that children first learn to categorize males and females, then they identify themselves as one or the other, and their identification then determines preference. If this sequence were also true for ethnic developments, we should find that a preference for one's own group correlates with identification with one's group. There is considerable evidence to support this prediction, although the picture is not as clear as one might hope.

Both ethnic preference and identification develop around the ages of 4 and 5. For White children, preference and identification are directed toward their own group. However, for minority children, there is no evidence of widespread preference for their own group until after 7 years, though identification was found to be present earlier. These general trends alert us to the possibility that preference and identification may not always coincide. The real answer to our question about the effect of identification on preference will come from studies that look at the relation between the two in individual children regardless of age. For example, Fu and Fogel (1982) correlated 5-year-olds' assignment of evaluative statements to a White and a Black person with their identification with one of these people. Attitude and identification were correlated for Black children but not for White children. On the other hand, Aboud (1980) found that among 5- to 7-year-old Black and White children, ingroup attitude correlated with only one of three measures of identification and the measure differed for Blacks and Whites. Black children liked their own group more if they perceived themselves to be most similar to a child from their group. Their attitude was unrelated to choosing Black as a self-label or to their overall perceived similarity to three Black children. In contrast, White children liked their own group more if they labelled themselves White. Their attitude was unrelated to perceptions of similarity to other White children. Perceived similarity was generally low in the 5-year-olds, possibly because of the overdiscrimination effect. This effect refers to the fact that young children give more weight to different attributes than to similar attributes when judging if two persons are similar or different. It has been noted on many occasions in the perceptual judgements of young children. Even the same person dressed differently is judged to be different from himself. This phenomenon raises the possibility that the formation of ethnic attitudes may be determined initially more by perceptions of difference from other ethnic groups than by the identification with one's own ethnic group. Because dissimilarity judgements are rarely included in ethnic research as a measure independent of ingroup indentification, it is difficult to test this idea.

When preference is not congruent with identification, what is the prevalent combination? Do children prefer their own group but not identify with it, or do they identify with their own group but not prefer it? Our conclusion in chapter 4 was that although most children identified with and preferred their own group, a number of children identified with but did not prefer their group. In other words, between the ages of 4 and 7, more Black and White children accurately identified with their group than preferred it. This does not necessarily mean that identification develops before preference, but rather that identification becomes tied to reality (i.e. actual ethnic background) before attitudes become pro-ingroup. This implies that in the early years, attitudes are not necessarily determined by identification.

A statistical procedure called the Guttman scalogram analysis can be used to determine whether identification becomes ingroup-directed before preferences. The analysis pays special attention to children who express incongruent judgements, such as an ingroup preference with no ingroup self-identification. Using this analysis, Aboud (1980) found that the ingroup preference of Black children preceded ingroup identification. The same pattern was found for White children with the exception of some who knew their ethnic label before they acquired ingroup preference, and some who strongly identified with their group but preferred others. The last pattern reflects the phenomenon discussed in chapter 3, namely that around 7 and 8 years many White children begin to express more positive outgroup attitudes even though they still identify with their own group. The order of acquisition of ingroup preference and identification may be reversed in this study, compared to the ones discussed previously, for a number of reasons. The point to be made, however, is that the two are not always congruent. The incongruency reveals that, at least in the early years from 4 to 7, preference is not entirely determined by the perceptual and cognitive processes of identification. Further studies using the Guttman scalogram or a longitudinal design will be necessary before we can say with certainty how preference is related to identification.

Self-identification has a more cognitive component, known as ethnic constancy, which may be related to the post-7 change in attitudes. Ethnic constancy refers to the understanding that a person's ethnicity remains the same despite transformations in superficial features. It is usually measured with hypothetical questions about a person who undergoes transformations or by showing the child pictures of a person in his/her original and his/her transformed state. Semaj (1980) asked the hypothetical questions of Black children between the ages of 4 and 11. The first question was, 'Can a Black child become a White child if she/he really wants to?' Seventy-five per cent of the children aged 4 and 5 said yes, but the percentage dropped dramatically in children 6 years and older. Most adults are surprised by such an answer, but it simply indicates that young children attach great importance to their affect and motivation. What they like and want can determine their identification, because at this age, identification is not firmly rooted in the objective reality of their ethnicity. The second question Semaj asked was, 'Can a Black child become a White child if she/he puts on a blond wig?' The third question was, 'Can a Black child become a White child if she/he changes the colour of her/his face with make-up?' In response to a skin colour change, most children (between 60 per cent and 75 per cent) from 4 to 9 years of age said the child could become a White child. In this case, the lack of ethnic constancy is due to the importance children attach to physical appearance. Ethnic identification at this age is based on what one sees; a person is White if he or she looks like a White and Black if he/she looks like a Black. Constancy in terms of understanding that ethnicity remains the same despite superficial changes was strongly evident only among the 10- and 11-year-olds.

Aboud and Skerry (1983) examined children's understanding of their own constant ethnicity by showing White children photographs of themselves before and after a clothing transformation. The children ranged in age from 5 to 9 years. Three photos were taken of them; one in their personal clothing, one in parka and leggings, and a final one in full Eskimo outdoor clothing. The children were asked several warm-up questions to help them focus on kinship rather than pretence as the basis for their subsequent self-identification. Finally, pointing to the 'Eskimo' photo, the examiner asked, 'What are you?' The task pitted children's perception of their Eskimo appearance against what they knew to be their ethnicity, namely Jewish Canadian. As in Semaj's study, only 30 per cent showed constancy by saying they were Jewish even though they looked Eskimo. By relating these constancy identifications to previously assessed descriptions of themselves and their ethnic group, we discovered some interesting connections. Those who understood their own constant identification possessed two mature cognitions that were not possessed by the nonconstant children. The first cognition was about an internal attribute of their ethnic group, such as a belief, a sense of pride and affection, or a preference. The salience of this internal attribute helped the children keep in mind their Jewish affiliation in spite of the external change. Recall that internal attributes are not prevalent in children's ethnic group descriptions until after 8 years. The second cognition was that social roles such as ethnicity were essential to their being themselves, that is, important for their self-identity. This cognition may provide the motivation for maintaining one's ethnic identification. In children from 5 to 9 years, both cognitions appeared to be necessary underpinnings to constancy. However, it is conceivable that the basis of constancy changes with age, that cognitions about internal attributes become a more important basis and that considering ethnicity essential to oneself becomes less important.

Other researchers have studied the understanding of ethnic constancy with similar results (e.g. Aboud, 1984; Doyle et al., 1987). This phenomenon is important for several reasons. One is that it reveals how lengthy is the process of developing a mature understanding of ethnic identification. Although children can identify their own and others' ethnicity at 4 or 5, they do not consider ethnicity to be an enduring part of the person until much later. Changes in attitude may accompany not only the initial identification of oneself and others, but also the later understanding of this identification. Another reason is that nonconstancy reveals how subjective is the basis of ethnicity in young children; for them, constancy is based on what they want or see. In contrast, 8-year-olds are beginning to understand that ethnicity has an objective basis in reality and exists independently of what the person thinks or feels. Perhaps this separation of ethnicity from other qualities of the person allows for a change in one's attitude to that ethnicity.

As was the case with the two previously discussed cognitions, constancy appears to be a concrete operational skill that depends on the acquisition of conservation as well as on other more mature cognitions. Its relation to ethnic attitudes is not clearly established. Doyle et al. found no relation between constancy and flexible evaluations of own and other ethnic groups. However, Semaj did find a connection. Among 4- to 7-year-old Black children, those with higher levels of constancy (obviously not very high at this age) expressed more pro-Black attitudes. Among 8- to 11-year-old Black children, those with higher levels of constancy expressed either pro-Black attitudes or equally high Black and White attitudes. For example, in response to the question, 'Which is better, Black or White?' the constancy children either said that Black was better or that both were equally good.

Summary. Three types of ethnic cognitions were shown to affect the child's understanding of ethnic differences and their own ethnic affiliation. One was cognitions about attributes possessed by ethnic groups and the heavy emphasis placed on external features such as skin and language. The second was an increase in flexibility evidenced by the ability to acknowledge that similar attributes can exist in ethnically different individuals and that different attributes can exist in ethnically similar individuals. The third was the understanding that ethnicity is constant and therefore has an objective basis independent of wishes or perceptions. These cognitions were found to change with age, particularly around the ages of 7 and 8 and often again three years later. They changed in the direction of giving more emphasis to internal qualities, perhaps at first the internal qualities of ethnic groups and then the internal qualities of individuals. These cognitions also allowed the child to make more distinctions between things: a distinction between external appearance and internal state, a distinction between what one wants to be and what one is, a distinction between attitude and cognitions. As a part of the overall cognitive development of the child, these three types of ethnic cognitions were related to and often preceded by the acquisition of cognitions about the physical world, such as conservation. These ethnic cognitions are also in some way related to prejudice. The full extent and the complex nature of this relation have yet to be clarified. However, the evidence that presently exists is promising: children who are aware of internal ethnic attributes, who have flexible ethnic cognitions and who understand the constancy of ethnicity tend to express less prejudice.

A SOCIAL-COGNITIVE DEVELOPMENTAL THEORY OF PREJUDICE

After reviewing research on the development of prejudice in children, I was struck by the changes that occurred at certain ages. It became clear that a full explanation of prejudice must take into account the capacities existing in the prejudiced person, and that the development of prejudice must take into account the development of these capacities. Because the capacities of a child differ from those of an adult, the explanations offered for prejudice in adults will not be adequate to explain prejudice in children. Thus, my initial assumption is that prejudice at different ages is based on different processes, and that the process which dominates a child's functioning at a particular age will also determine his/her ethnic attitudes.

The notion that different processes underlie prejudice at different ages is not unusual. Zanna and Rempel (in press) have proposed that even among adults different processes may underlie different attitudes. The processes they describe are affect, perception of behaviour and cognition – the three components often cited in definitions of attitude. Zanna and Rempel make a strong case for viewing them not as components of an attitude, because this prejudges the question of whether they are indeed related, but rather as potential sources of an attitude. Any process singly or in combination with others may be the basis of an attitude, which they define as simply an evaluation. This is compatible with my own developmental view of ethnic attitudes, if one adds the assumption that one of these processes may dominate the child's functioning and thus form the basis of prejudice at a particular age.

The developmental sequence in which these processes dominate attitude formation is first affect, then perception and finally cognition. Specifically, in the early years affective processes such as emotions and needs determine the child's attitudes toward their own and other ethnic groups. Following this, perceptual processes such as the perception of one's own and others' appearance and behaviour influence the child's attitudes. Finally, after the age of 7 or 8, cognitive processes such as the ones discussed at the beginning of this chapter influence the child's attitudes. This sequence from affective to perceptual to cognitive functioning has some support from the developmental literature generally as well as from the ethnic attitude literature. In particular, the strengthening of cognitive understanding from the age of 7 on is widely recognized. In many different ways, the child's cognitive capacities expand. For example, children are able to attend to more than one dimension at a time; they can think and solve problems abstractly; they can infer qualities of people and objects that are not directly observable; and they can even think about their own capacities and about their limitations in relation to other people and other points of view. These developments have been studied in comparison with the pre-7 child who lacks these capacities and who therefore is more dependent on other processes such as affective and perceptual ones.

Affective and perceptual determinants of prejudice.   The dominance of affective processes in the early years is still somewhat controversial. Piagetian theory described the preoperational child in terms of being dependent on perceptual, sensory and motor processes. However, in his theory of preference, Zajonc (1980) claims that affective processes are in a sense more primitive than cognition and perception, and can exist independently of them. Zajonc cites evidence to suggest that the encoding of affects or preferences is more similar to the encoding of motor events than of cognitive events. One's affective reaction to a stimulus is immediate, inevitable and intense; it may be based on minimal perception and cognition of the stimulus; and its retrieval occurs without effort. This means that emotions and preferences are strong, immediate and easily triggered again by the same object or person. Because emotions and preferences are strong and immediate, we take them to be the correct reactions under such circumstances. In addition, because emotions and preferences occur with little cognitive work, they are rarely examined or changed even in the face of contradictory information.

The view that emotional reactions dominate the young child's functioning has some support even from cognitive developmental theories. Take, for example, Kohlberg's (1976) moral development theory. Kohlberg proposes six stages in the development of moral judgement. The first two are referred to as preconventional in the sense that they are pre-social. Children from 4 to 7 years typically make judgements that are preconventional. At the first stage, children determine right and wrong on the basis of the external consequences of their actions such as rewards and punishments. At the second stage, something is right if it satisfies their needs and gives them pleasure and is wrong if it gives them pain. In both cases, the evaluation is based on an affective or emotional reaction, though at first this reaction is tied to the concrete rewards and punishments given by adults. Children at the conventional stages base their evaluations on social rules, or rules laid down by authority figures. This clearly requires more cognitive understanding of social groups and the notion of rules.

It is interesting to note that the need for approval, discussed in chapter 6, is inversely related to moral stage. Independent of age, children at the preconventional stages of moral development have more need for approval than children at the conventional stages (Tracy and Cross, 1973). Thus, in the early years, children are concerned mainly with need satisfaction, and with pleasure and pain. The need to feel approved, good and happy manifests itself in several ways. One is that children from 4 to 7 years typically have an overly positive evaluation of themselves (Harter and Pike, 1984) and deny sadness and other socially undesirable experiences in themselves. They avoid and dislike peers who are not approved or who experience dissatisfaction (Glasberg and Aboud, 1981; Madge, 1976).

The important question for our purposes is what emotional states underlie the young child's positive and negative attitudes, and what elicits these emotions. Two strong and early emotions in the child that underlie avoidance and approach tendencies are fear and attachment. Young children are typically afraid of what is unknown and what is different. When it is a person rather than an object that is unknown and different, the fear is likely to persist. This is because young children possess some exploratory skills which allow them to become familiar with and control a novel object but which are not appropriately used with people. Instead, with a novel person they tend to maintain their distance and to observe. Attachment is elicited by people who give the child a sense of security and comfort. It is a strong emotional bond, which is usually mutual but not symmetrical in the way it is experienced. The mutual component is what we usually refer to as love; the asymmetrical component is similar to respect. The latter component arises because the child feels attachment for an adult who provides security and comfort, and thus possesses qualities that the child needs but does not yet have. Children experience both fear and attachment by 8 months of age, and although the emotions become more focused and complex with age, they are nonetheless strong social emotions during the child's early years.

Children who initially form a strong preference for their own group and prejudice toward other groups are simply generalizing their attachment/respect for their parents to other people who look similar, and experiencing fear toward people who are different and less known. Children habitually externalize their fear by saying that there is something threatening or bad about the person who elicits their fear.

Children who initially form a strong preference for an outgroup such as Whites are probably generalizing the respect they have for their parents' qualities to people they assume must also possess these qualities, rather than to people who simply look similar to their parents. Because of their interpretation of the status differences perceived in their preschool classroom or in the media, they assume that Whites possess the qualities that result in security, approval and happiness more than do members of their own group. It is unlikely that fear underlies their lesser preference for their own group; rather, the emotion may be respect but at a lower level. Fear probably underlies their prejudice for another outgroup that is different and unknown, such as when Native Indians dislike Blacks or Blacks dislike Asians.

The dominance of affective processes brings along with it a focus on the self. Not only emotional states and needs, but also the child's perception of an event are very salient to him/her. This has been referred to as egocentrism and is thought to arise from natural cognitive limitations. It has been explained in terms of the inability to differentiate or decentrate. Before the age of 7, children cannot control their own salient perspective on an event enough to attend to someone else's different perspective. The shift to perceptual and cognitive functioning appears to be followed by a shift in focus away from oneself and toward groups and later individuals. The change in orientation from self to groups to individuals is not new to developmental theory. Although the change in focus is not directly tied to the affective-cognitive change, the two sequences undoubtedly overlap and together could lay the framework for a social-cognitive developmental theory of prejudice. Together the two sequences could explain what psychological processes form the bases of prejudice and what social factors are going to be most influential at a particular age. Because self-centred affective processes form the basis of early attitudes, social factors that address these emotions and needs will be most influential. That is, only social forces that directly impinge on the child will be influential. Moreover, parental attitudes and the values of favourite book or TV characters will be reinterpreted in terms of the child's concerns with attachment, fear, reward and approval. Evaluations and preferences will develop consistent with these affective states.

Although self-centred affective processes seem to dominate the child from 4 to 7 years, it is clear that perceptual processes begin at this age to have a strong input. Children of this age attend more to the observable features than to the internal attributes of themselves and other ethnic group members. For example, they ethnically identify people on the basis of their appearance and regardless of their ancestry. Also, perceptions of similarity are based on specific features and not on ethnicity per se. That is why children of this age will often say that they are similar to some members of their own group and different from others. These examples reveal that children from 5 to 7 years rely more on their perceptions than on their cognitions. At this age also, the focus of attention shifts from self to groups. Children whose judgements are dominated by their perceptual processes focus on the observable differences between groups. These polarized perceptions spill over into attitudes, so that the statement 'I see the two groups differently' translates into 'I like the two groups differently'. It is difficult to say how perceptual processes develop with respect to the affective processes described previously. My feeling is that in the social domain, affective processes dominate from 3 to 6 years and then decline. Perceptual processes develop during these years sometimes outweighing the affective response, and dominate from 6 to 7 or 8 years.

Cognitive determinants of prejudice.   The real shift to cognitive functioning begins around 7 years of age and continues to increase over the next 3 or 4 years. Conservation and perspective taking, two benchmarks of concrete operational thinking, are usually firmly in place by 8 years of age. However, other cognitive skills such as understanding internal states and flexible ethnic cognitions continue to improve substantially during the years from 8 to 12. It seems likely then that the initial cognitive developments allow children to understand the concept of groups, and that later cognitive developments facilitate an understanding of individual differences. When children are preoccupied with group categorization, their self-identification and their attitudes will largely be determined by their own and others' group membership. When children become more attentive to unique individual qualities, their self-identification may include attributes that are inconsistent with their group membership and their attitudes will be based more on an individual's nonethnic qualities.

The striking development of cognitive structures around 7 and 8 years of age was discussed earlier in this chapter. The transition from preoperational to concrete operational thinking which occurs at this time signals the change from affective and perceptual dominance to cognitive dominance. This change has been fully documented by Flavell (1977) in both the physical and social domains. In the ethnic domain specifically, there are at least three types of cognitions whose development appears to depend on the development of physical cognitions and which are in turn related to prejudice. The three, described previously, are cognitions about the internal attributes and preferences of ethnic groups, flexible cognitions that minimize group differences and maximize individual differences, and the understanding of ethnic constancy. These three ethnic cognitions appear to depend for their development on the understanding of conservation of matter, a critical index of concrete operational thinking. Furthermore, their development appears to follow conservation, indicating that additional, more mature cognitions are also necessary. These additional cognitions have not yet been isolated, but they could be specific to ethnic content or more generally related to social and cognitive development.

With respect to flexible cognitions about ethnic groups, for example, major shifts occurred at two critical ages. Shifts toward minimizing group differences occurred just prior to 8 years and 12 years according to Doyle et al. (1987). The critical age for maximizing individual differences was 12 years according to Katz et al. It appears that children are preoccupied with groups, first with their differences and then with their similarities, before they become aware of the unique qualities of individuals who make up these groups. Although the two processes overlap and although minimizing group differences may contribute to maximizing individual differences, it seems likely that children's attention to groups precedes their attention to individuals. An additional cognition necessary to enhance attention to individual differences is the awareness and salience of internal qualities such as emotions, thoughts, goals and traits.

Ethnic constancy, like flexibility, depends on and follows the development of conservation. In a sense, it is not surprising that in order to understand the invariance of ethnicity, one must first understand the invariance of matter. However, as with flexibility, there may be several overlapping levels to constancy. The first is to understand that ethnic identity remains constant despite one's desires. Semaj (1980) found many 4- and 5-year-olds who said that people could change their ethnicity from Black to White if they wanted to. The mature form of constancy is to understand that ethnicity remains the same despite changes in appearance because ethnicity is based on unobservable qualities such as ancestry or genetics. Some children say that ethnicity remains the same but their explanation is based on inflexible group categorization rather than on internal qualities. That is, they say that a White person must always be White because that is the rule and one would always be able to find an external feature that gave them away – their leg would be white or their speech would be white. It is important to distinguish among the different levels of constancy. At the first level the child believes that ethnic identity is whatever one wants to be. At the second level the child bases identity on rigid categorization or external appearance. At the third level the child bases identity on internal factors (Aboud and Ruble, 1987). The first level corresponds to self-centred affective functioning. The second corresponds to perceptual dominance or to cognitive functioning with an emphasis on groups. The third corresponds to cognitive functioning with an emphasis on internal qualities.

These three ethnic cognitions are in turn related in some way to ethnic attitudes. They seem to be associated with lower levels of prejudice and perhaps with the decline in ethnocentrism noted in children over 8 years. As described previously, Doyle et al. and Katz et al. found lower levels of prejudice in White children who perceived minimal group differences and maximal individual differences. Lower levels of prejudice in Black children were associated with some perception of individual differences but not with a minimizing of group differences (Katz et al., 1975). Davidson (1976) found lower levels of prejudice in children who gave higher levels of moral judgement and who used fewer concrete descriptors of ethnic groups.

Shift from self to group and individual focus. Overlapping the change from affective and perceptual functioning to cognitive functioning is the shift from a focus on self to a focus on groups and then individuals. Affective functioning seems to be characteristic of the egocentric or self-centred child whose own perspective and own satisfactions are more salient than those of anyone else. At this age, children's perceptions of other people are largely influenced by how that person relates to them. However, when children decentrate, their focus of attention appears to broaden to include groups of people. Oneself and others are perceived in terms of the groups or categories to which they belong. Only later are children able to attend to the unique qualities of individuals, namely to the internal and consistent characteristics of a person that make them different from others. Clearest evidence for the shift from group to individual focus comes from the research by Doyle et al. (1987) and Katz et al. (1975) in which children initially maximized ethnic group differences, then minimized group differences, and finally maximized individual differences of members within a group.

This shift in attention from self to groups to individuals underlies two other theories of social development, namely Block's theory of sex-role development and Kohlberg's theory of moral judgement. Thus, it may represent changes in general cognitive development associated with the ability increasingly to differentiate among entities, and not changes in ethnic attitudes only. In the early stages of sex-role development (Block, 1973), children are thought to identify themselves and adopt behaviours according to their own wishes and satisfactions. In the middle stages, children are preoccupied with social rules which define the relevant groups and prescibe appropriate behaviours for these groups. To children of this age, it is important that people be identified in terms of their gender and that they closely follow the rules of conduct for males and females. In the later stages, children come to see that rules are flexible and that individuals must take responsibility for deciding what behaviours are most suited to their individual needs and personalities. They also accept that someone else may decide differently from themselves. At the final stage, a person's gender identity is secure enough to allow him or her to adopt behaviours seen as more characteristic of the opposite sex. This sequence from self to social group to individual focus of attention is found in moral development as well (Kohlberg, 1976). Scores on tests designed to measure one's level of sex-role and moral development correlate, indicating that something in common underlies the two sequences of development. As yet no studies have correlated scores on either of these tests with a measure of flexible ethnic cognitions, but I would predict that they correlate highly.

Applied to the ethnic domain, the first stage involves a preoccupation with oneself and one's satisfactions. People will be identified with and liked to the extent that they possess resources to satisfy one's needs. At this stage, children are not strongly influenced by other people. The second stage is characterized by a preoccupation with oneself as a group member. One identifies with and likes the group to which one belongs. Other group members are seen only in terms of their belonging to a different group. Social rules determine how one reacts to each group. Thus, children at this stage are more strongly influenced by parent and peer attitudes because these represent rules. Also, because rules govern preferences, certain preferences are right and others are wrong. The third stage involves an emphasis on oneself and others as individuals again, but now with a more differentiated and internal perspective. One identifies with many social groups and in terms of many personal attributes regardless of their seeming incompatibility. That is, one may identify with ingroup members because they possess the same ethnic background but identify with other ethnic group members who hold the same educational values. Likewise, other people are perceived in terms not only of their ethnic group but also of their personality. Attitudes toward people are based on their individual dispositions rather than their group membership. Presumably, not everyone develops to this stage of ethnic identity and attitude, just as not everyone develops an androgynous sex role. At this stage, one is influenced more by one's own personal knowledge of the other person, or by people whom one considers to be knowledgeable. That is, someone from another ethnic group who is familiar with that group might have a greater influence on one's attitudes than someone from one's own group who is not familiar with such people. Close friend relationships might also be influential.

This sequence applies most clearly to majority children who initially acquire ingroup preference and identity rather than outgroup preference. It seems to apply equally well to the development of a new identity in initially pro-White Blacks. Cross (1980, 1987) described five stages of Black identity, three of which correspond to Block's (1973). The Pre-encounter stage entails White identification and preference. The Immersion stage is characterized by a high level of Black identification and glorification along with a strong dislike of Whites. In the Internalization stage, one identifies with Blacks internally and more confidently. Attitudes toward Whites as a group become less negative and friendship with a White individual is possible. Presumably this description could apply to any minority person who initially prefers Whites, and to child as well as adult development. The Encounter stage is distinctive to minority identification and is the turning point from being pro-White to pro-ingroup. Cross describes the catalyst as 'a shocking personal or social event'. For an adult, the event may be a vivid experience of being discriminated against; for a child, it may be the cognition that ethnic identity is based on physical features or family rather than wishful thinking.

It may be possible to pinpoint what stages of the outlined sequence are expected to be highly prejudiced ones. Firstly, children in the self-focused affective stage could be expected to hold highly polarized and prejudiced attitudes. Children who are group-focused but without much cognitive understanding are also likely to hold prejudiced attitudes. The decline in prejudice is associated with a breakdown in the polarized perception of group differences. Once children begin to notice some similarities between their own and other ethnic groups, they will be less prejudiced toward the others. This phase occurs well before children are able to fully appreciate individual differences, which according to Katz et al. (1975) and other studies of person perception, does not take place until 10 or 12 years. Minimizing group differences has already begun by 8 years. That is, children of 8 years are still probably preoccupied with the notion of groups, but they are starting to notice that groups are not as rigidly different as they thought. This would suggest that there is a major change occurring in the midst of the group-focus stage. In the early part of this stage, the emphasis on groups is based on perceptual rather than cognitive processes; differences rather than similarities are attended to. In the later part of this stage, the emphasis on groups is based on cognitive processes and so children are able to entertain more complex possibilities. One of these is that people who look different may be similar in some respects. This idea continues to expand over the next four years in the direction of both differences and similarities. The idea is then extended to incorporate the fact that people who look the same may be different in some respects. This is when the focus on individuals becomes stronger. Both types of judgement, group similarities and individual differences, require an awareness of the distinction between external and internal qualities, but the latter clearly requires a fuller knowledge of internals. Although the 7-year watershed in prejudice probably occurs when cognition takes over from perception during the group stage, prejudice would be expected to decline further during the individual-focus stage.

The complex sequence of developments taking place after 7 years helps to explain why ethnic attitudes take so many different forms in the years prior to adolescence. The one common theme is that most children express some preference for their own group. This is explained in terms of the functioning of perceptual/cognitive processes that allow for an identification of oneself and one's family realistically as members of a particular ethnic group, and the cognitive need to hold evaluations consistent with one's perceptions. Beyond this common ingroup preference, there is a great deal of variability among individuals within an ethnic group as to the polarity of their likes and dislikes. Even though all these individuals are functioning at the concrete operational level, they may vary in the extent to which perceptions rather than cognitions and groups rather than individuals dominate their ethnic judgements. Those whose judgements are dominated by group-focused perceptions will attend to ethnic group differences and hold more polarized attitudes. Those whose judgements are dominated by group-focused cognitions will attend more to ethnic group similarities and hold less polarized attitudes. Least prejudiced will be those who are attentive to internal and unique individual qualities. In addition to their ethnic judgements being group or individual focused, children of this age are more responsive to social forces in their community, either in the form of group rules and norms or in the form of a credible individual's judgement. If a child of 10 years is surrounded by prejudiced family and friends, these social forces may encourage him/her to maintain a strong prejudice in spite of newly developing cognitive capabilities that would allow him/her to hold less prejudiced attitudes. If a child is surrounded by less prejudiced family and friends, then social forces would be working in the same direction as cognitive developments to reduce prejudice. In both cases, the child has a choice because cognitive capabilities and social influences are less limiting, less restrictive than they were in the pre-7 years. The choice is to interpret ethnic differences in a cognitively more mature and flexible way, or to interpret them in the more polarized and prejudiced way of certain social forces. When cognitive and social forces pull the child in opposite directions with equal strength, the choice is clearly more difficult.

SUMMARY OF MAJOR POINTS OF THE THEORY

The proposed social-cognitive developmental theory of prejudice assumes that age-related changes in ethnic attitudes are related to the development of certain capacities. Two sequences of development, thought to underlie general cognitive and social development, are proposed to underlie the development of prejudice. One sequence relates to a change in the process that dominates the child's functioning – from affective and perceptual processes to cognitive processes. The second sequence relates to a change in the focus of one's attention – from self, to group, to individual focus. These two sequences overlap to a large extent. When affective processes dominate, the child will be most attentive to self concerns. When perceptual processes dominate, attention will be focused on groups. Finally, when cognitive processes dominate, the child will attend first to groups and then shift over to individuals.

Although prejudice begins during the affective self-centred stage, one would expect more consensus and more polarization of attitudes during the stage when group differences are paramount. A decline in prejudice would be expected at the age when cognitive capabilities allow one to minimize group differences and notice group similarities. Further reductions in prejudice would be expected at the age when cognitive capabilities allow one to attend to individual differences within groups. Thus, the potential for less polarized attitudes depends on cognitive development as it relates to group and then to individual focus. The sequence from affective to cognitive functioning also predicts that in the early years, attitudes and wishes determine one's identity, whereas after 7 years, ethnic self-identification partly determines attitudes. The sequence of attention from self to group to individual underlies how the child perceives him or herself and others. It also probably determines what kind of information the child will be sensitive to, i.e. what factors influence the child's attitudes. Social factors would be expected to be less influential in the early years when self-satisfactions are important, and more influential in the middle stage when groups are critical. This in fact was the case in many studies where parental attitudes and school integration had a much stronger influence on children over 7 or 8 years than on younger children. In the last stage, only selected social factors such as those endowed with respect and expertise would be expected to have an influence.

The major weakness of this framework is that it does not allow for a clear prediction of the direction of preference at the affective-self stage. Although one might expect ingroup members to be seen as happy and receiving approval and other desirable resources, and therefore to be preferred, many minority group children prefer outgroup Whites over their own group. There is a great deal of heterogeneity in the 4- to 7-year-old Black samples reported here, but more pro-White consensus among the other minority samples. The pro-White preferences of these young children coincide with the social values of their societies. The question is, From where are they receiving the information on this value and how are they interpreting it? Why do only some children become aware of this value, or interpret it in terms their needs? Although many people point to community and parent values as the mediators between society and children, the evidence is not strong. In particular the study by Branch and Newcombe (1986) found that pro-Black parents had pro-White children of 4 and 5 years. Presumably the children were interpreting their parents' attitude and belief statements in a way that was different from what the parents intended. Consequently, it remains a puzzle how to explain or predict the direction of minority children's preferences in the 4 to 7 age range.

The strength of this framework is that it explains age-related changes in ethnic attitudes. It accounts for the development of prejudice in terms of the development of processes known to be influential in social development generally. In particular, it explains striking developmental changes that occur after 7 years of age, and that are not explained by other theories of prejudice. These changes are attributed to the development of perceptual and then cognitive capabilities that allow for a shift in focus from self to groups to individuals. Aspects of prejudice common to most children as well as individual differences can be dealt with by these two overlapping sequences of development because both the degree of polarization of ingroup–outgroup attitudes and the range of social forces to which the child is sensitive change with development.

Rather than condemning other theories of prejudice, I might argue that the social reflection theories are valid, but for a limited age period. The importance of social values that are tied to power and status may be valid between the ages of 4 and 7 if a child has no strong self-identification and if affective/motivational satisfactions dominate preferences. The importance of parental and group values emphasizing ingroup–outgroup contrasts might be salient only after the age of 7 when perceptual processes with a group focus have come to dominate preferences. Neither social theory goes beyond this developmental stage. A lack of prejudice is explained in terms of a lack of these value systems in the society, rather than in terms of more mature developments in the child.

A Note to Educators

Many adults are disturbed when they see or hear an incident of prejudice or interethnic conflict among children. Children we know to be happy and loving may quite openly say something derogatory about the ethnicity of a classmate. We may overhear their fabricated gossip about an ethnically different child. Or we may see them exclude, tease or bully a child for explicit ethnic reasons. To parents who consider themselves tolerant of ethnic differences, it is confusing and disturbing to see one's own child be so intolerant. To a teacher who implicitly and explicitly maintains a tolerant attitude toward ethnic groups, it is disappointing to see none of this rubbing off on the class.

People often blame a child's prejudice on the parents. They assume that the parents are prejudiced and teach these attitudes to their child. This is unjustified. Pre-7 children do not adopt their parents' attitudes and are often more prejudiced than their parents. Post-7 children are influenced by their parents but not solely by them. Other factors shape attitudes too. Most parents, however, are not aware that the accusation is unjustified, and so are sensitive to any suggestion that their child may be prejudiced. They tend to resist any testing of their child's attitudes and any intervention aimed at reducing prejudice.

For a number of reasons, however, school intervention programmes are desirable. I am referring here to curriculum programmes aimed at reducing prejudice; integrated schooling programmes are another issue entirely. Firstly, prejudice seems to be prevalent among White children in the years from 4 to 7 (and probably also among minority children in their attitudes toward other minorities). Secondly, although beginning at 7 years children are cognitively capable of being less prejudiced, they may choose to be influenced by prejudiced parents and peers, or they may not have the exposure to information which allows them to use their newly developed cognitive capabilities. A golden opportunity might be lost if children were not given the chance to exercise these new capabilities with the appropriate kind of information about ethnic groups.

A number of activities have been shown to reduce prejudice. The reasons why they do not prevent prejudice is that they are not effective at an early enough age to prevent prejudice from forming in the first place, and though they may reduce prejudice they do not often eliminate it entirely. Except for school desegregation programmes (Schofield, 1986), most of these activities, unfortunately, have been implemented in classrooms or camps in a very controlled manner. Trained professionals have taken a small group of children and exposed them to a short but concentrated programme of information. The adults running the programme are well motivated and trained to eliminate any information that is extraneous or counter to the programme. These programmes are useful in demonstrating exactly what information and activities reduce prejudice. However, they are not easy to implement on a large scale and not suitable for use in the classroom. One good example of such a programme is described by Katz and Zalk (1978).

Instead, I will describe a programme that follows from the developmental theory of prejudice proposed in chapter 7. This theory suggests that different factors are responsible for maintaining and therefore for reducing prejudice at different ages. Working with an organization called Alternatives to Racism in Vancouver, Canada, my colleague Anna Beth Doyle and I came up with three propositions that we considered relevant for the 7- to 12-year age range. They were the following:

1 Judging people on the basis of internal rather than external attributes increases with age and is inversely related to prejudice.
2 Attending to between-group similarities and within-group differences increases with age and is inversely related to prejudice.
3 Recognizing that one's own perspective may differ from another's and that both these perspectives can be valid increases with age and facilitates an acceptance of ethnic differences.

Guided by these propositions, Jack Kehoe from the University of British Columbia and his co-workers Diane Swanson and Vivien Bowers (1988) produced an educational unit for fifth-grade students. The unit consists of eleven activities, some to be completed by the class as a whole and some to be completed by each student individually. The activities were designed to be fun for the students, to arouse their interest and their involvement. They were also designed with the teacher in mind, because the teacher must feel comfortable and competent with the material in order to discuss it sensitively. Teachers were also requested to assess the general school climate toward ethnic tolerance in terms of such things as flexible school procedures, honouring specific ethnic individuals and events, and facilitating cross-ethnic interaction inside and outside the classroom.

The objectives of the programme are generally to reduce prejudice and stereotyping. Specifically, they are to make cross-ethnic interaction a positive experience, to encourage the development of interaction skills, and to promote acceptance of both group and individual differences. To accomplish these objectives, the activities give children practice in the three processes described previously: judging people on the basis of internal rather than external attributes; attending to between-group similarities and within-group differences; recognizing that two different perspectives may both be valid.

The role of the teacher is twofold. Firstly, the teacher is a facilitator and discussion leader. By providing a provoking and open atmosphere, the teacher invites children to express comfortably their opinions and evaluations. The purpose of the discussions is to explore different points of view so that the children themselves can learn to evaluate objectively their own desirable and undesirable reactions to ethnic differences. Secondly, the teacher also becomes a model and diplomat in setting the tone of acceptance and in valuing culturally different ways of experiencing this world.

The unit is entitled More Than Meets the Eye and consists of three sections: understanding yourself, understanding others and understanding differences. The first two sections give the children practice at emphasizing internal qualities and at differentiating members within groups. The third section gives children practice in detecting, explaining and generating examples of occasions when different perspectives are valid.

Understanding Yourself is the title of the first set of activities. These activities give the children practice at emphasizing internal qualities and at differentiating members within their own ethnic group. For example, the children first complete their own personal profile, including external features such as height and colouring and internal qualities such as abilities, emotions and preferences. They then compare their profile with that of a friend and a lesser-known classmate to note similarities and differences. The teacher asks them to identify qualities in others that are either strange and unlikeable or pleasantly surprising. The children then discuss these reactions and how one can learn to accept both kinds of qualities and reactions.

Understanding Others is the title of the second set of activities. These activities give the children practice at emphasizing internal qualities and at differentiating between members of the same ethnic group. However, this time the focus is on children from several different ethnic groups, collectively called the Hoozhoo Kids. These are 30 actual fifth-grade children whose profiles appear on the back of their individual photos. For example, one boy is described as:

Good at hockey, driving mom up the wall
Poor at cleaning his room, wrestling
Likes comics, sleep
Hates school, broccoli
Worries about mom working too hard
Wants to be a team manager
Personality: acts lazy and rude, can be kind and helpful.

One of the girls' profiles reads as follows:

Good at writing poems, dancing
Poor at math, remembering things
Likes earrings, computers
Hates some boys, colour green
Worries about scary movies
Wants to be a professional dancer
Personality: imaginative and creative, loves to read.

A number of games are offered in which children practise associating names of the Hoozhoo Kids with their faces, and with their profiles. For example, children are given black and white pictures of each Kid showing only half the face. They must draw in the other half and write the name underneath. A crossword puzzle of Kids' names can be completed using clues which describe something about the Kid's personality, preferences or abilities.

Finally, the section entitled Understanding Differences consists of a set of activities which give children practice at identifying, explaining and generating their own examples of instances where two different perspectives are both valid. Discussion focuses on how ethnic group and individual characteristics can explain these different perspectives. In contrast, there are other instances where society does not respect differing points of view, and for these instances we have rules. Some activities deal with ways in which the student's feelings differ from other family members and friends, and ways in which the student's feelings differ from members of other ethnic groups. Another activity called Choose Your Own Fun requires children to complete a maze by making choices based on their own personal preferences for food and fun. Different routes all reach the goal at the end labelled Good Time.

More than Meets the Eye is a unit which helps to develop the ethnic cognitions of 10-year-old children. It could probably be used in a slightly modified form with children as young as 7 or 8 years because it is based on three principles which apply to the 7- to 12-year range. However, it is not appropriate for children younger than 7. Between 4 and 7 years, children's attitudes are not strongly influenced by their cognitions and the ethnic cognitions in question are not easily grasped.

If I were to design a unit for children between 4 and 7 years, it would have to be based on a different set of propositions, which at this point are reasonable but largely untested. For example:

1 Prejudice is based on a polarized and simple dichotomy of positive versus negative emotions. A greater differentiation among emotions reduces prejudice.
2 Prejudice is based on an egocentric judgement that only one way of experiencing the world is the correct way. Learning the many ways of being right reduces prejudice.

One objective, then, would be to broaden the range of emotions the children are aware of experiencing, and to broaden the range of emotions they feel secure in expressing to different ethnic persons. Most children at this age think of emotions as being either positive or negative, i.e. pleasant or unpleasant. They make few distinctions among positive emotions such as satisfied, happy, loving, liking, eager, surprised; and few distinctions among negative emotions such as afraid, sad, angry, lonely, disappointed, confused and worried. They see few similarities between a positive and a negative emotion. A second objective would be to teach the children culturally different ways of living and to let them egocentrically and vicariously identify with the happiness and attachments of children from different cultures.

The kind of curriculum unit I am referring to here follows a tradition that is based on the assumption that information reduces prejudice. Many such programmes have been tried and tested in various settings (e.g. Bunton and Weissbach, 1974; Crooks, 1970; Likover, 1971). To a certain extent, they have resulted in a reduction of prejudice in White children and an enhancement of ingroup attachment in minority children. There are two major differences in the programmes I have described. One is that they are geared to the age-related concerns of the child – to the process that is dominant (affective or cognitive) and to the focus of attention (self, groups, individuals). The programme for 4- to 7-year-olds emphasizes self-focused affective concerns. The programme for 7- to 12-year-olds emphasizes group- and individual-focused cognitive concerns. The second difference is that the programmes give the child an opportunity to practise newly developed or developing capabilities as they apply to ethnic issues. The programmes, therefore, combine exposure to information about ethnic members as well as skill development. Skill development is a new idea in this area because educators have typically taken a social psychological rather than a social–cognitive developmental approach to prejudice. The latter is probably more compatible with their professional views of child development. Given that educators are familiar with both the theories of cognitive development and the strategies of skill development, they could make a major and lasting contribution to the reduction of prejudice.

References

Aboud, F.E. (1976). Self-evaluation: Information-seeking strategies for inter-ethnic social comparisons. *Journal of Cross-Cultural Psychology, 7,* 289–300.

Aboud, F.E. (1977). Interest in ethnic information: A cross-cultural developmental study. *Canadian Journal of Behavioural Science, 9,* 134–46.

Aboud, F.E. (1980). A test of ethnocentrism with young children. *Canadian Journal of Behavioural Science, 12,* 195–209.

Aboud, F.E. (1981). Egocentrism, conformity, and agreeing to disagree. *Developmental Psychology, 17,* 791–99.

Aboud, F.E. (1984). Social and cognitive bases of ethnic identity constancy. *Journal of Genetic Psychology, 184,* 217–30.

Aboud, F.E. and Christian, J.D. (1979). Development of ethnic identity. In L. Eckensberger, Y. Poortinga and W.J. Lonner (eds.), *Cross–cultural contributions to psychology.* Lisse, Holland: Swets and Zeitlinger.

Aboud, F.E. and Mitchell, F.G. (1977). Ethnic role taking: The effects of preference and self-identification. *International Journal of Psychology, 12,* 1–17.

Aboud, F.E. and Ruble, D.N. (1987). Identity constancy in children: Developmental processes and implications. In T.M. Honess and K.M. Yardley (eds.), *Self and identity: Individual change and development.* London: Routledge and Kegan Paul.

Aboud, F.E. and Skerry, S.A. (1983). Self and ethnic concepts in relation to ethnic constancy. *Canadian Journal of Behavioural Science, 15,* 14–26.

Adam, J. (1978). Sequential strategies and the separation of age, cohort, and time-of-measurement contributions to developmental data. *Psychological Bulletin, 85,* 1309–16.

Adorno, T.W., Frenkel–Brunswick, E., Levinson, D.J. and Sanford, R.N. (1950). *The authoritarian personality.* New York: Harper and Row.

Allport, G.W. (1954). *The nature of prejudice.* Cambridge, Mass.: Addison–Wesley.

Asher, S.R. and Allen, V.L. (1969). Racial preference and social comparison processes. *Journal of Social Issues, 25,* 157–67.

Bagley C., Mallick K. and Verma G.K. (1979). Pupil self-esteem: A study of Black and White teenagers in British schools. In G.K. Verma and C. Bagley (eds.), *Race, education and identity.* London: Macmillan.

Bagley C., Verma G., Mallick K. and Young L. (1979). *Personality, self-esteem and prejudice*. England: Saxon House.

Bagley C. and Young L. (1979). The identity, adjustment and achievement of transracially adopted children: A review and empirical report. In G.K. Verma and C. Bagley (eds.), *Race, education and identity*. London: Macmillan.

Bandura, A., Ross, D. and Ross, S.A. (1963). A comparative test of the status envy, social power, and secondary reinforcement theories of identificatory learning. *Journal of Abnormal and Social Psychology, 67*, 527–34.

Banks, W.C. (1976). White preference in Blacks: A paradigm in search of a phenomenon. *Psychological Bulletin, 83*, 1179–86.

Banks, W.C. and Rompff, W.J. (1973). Evaluative bias and preference in Black and White children. *Child Development, 44*, 776–83.

Barnes, E.J. (1980). The Black community as the source of positive self-concept for Black children: A theoretical perspective. In R.L. Jones (ed.), *Black Psychology*. New York: Harper and Row.

Berry, J.W., Kalin, R. and Taylor, D.M. (1976). *Multiculturalism and ethnic attitudes in Canada*. Ottawa: Supply and Services.

Block, J.H. (1973). Conceptions of sex-role: Some cross-cultural and longitudinal perspectives. *American Psychologist, 28*, 512–26.

Bowers, V. and Swanson, D. (1988). *More than meets the eye*. Vancouver: Pacific Educational Press.

Branch, C.W. and Newcombe, N. (1980). Racial attitudes of Black preschoolers as related to parental civil rights activism. *Merrill–Palmer Quarterly, 26*, 425–8.

Branch, C.W. and Newcombe, N. (1986). Racial attitude development among young Black children as a function of parental attitudes: a longitudinal and cross-sectional study. *Child Development, 57*, 712–21.

Brand, E.S., Ruiz, R.A. and Padilla, A.M. (1974). Ethnic identification and preference: A review. *Psychological Bulletin, 81*, 860–90.

Brewer, M.B. (1979). Ingroup bias in the minimal intergroup situation: a cognitive motivational analysis. *Psychological Bulletin, 86*, 307–24.

Brown, G. and Johnson, S.P. (1971) The attribution of behavioural connotations to shaded and white figures by Caucasian children. *British Journal of Social and Clinical Psychology, 10*, 306–12.

Bunton, P.L. and Weissbach, T.A. (1974). Attitudes toward blackness of Black preschool children attending community-controlled or public schools. *Journal of Social Psychology, 92*, 53–9.

Clark, A., Hocevar, D. and Dembo, M.H. (1980). The role of cognitive development in children's explanations and preferences for skin color. *Developmental Psychology, 16*, 332–9.

Clark, K.B. and Clark, M.P. (1947). Racial identification and preference in Negro children. In T.M. Newcomb and E.L. Hartley (eds.), *Readings in social psychology*. New York: Holt, pp. 169–78.

Corenblum, B. and Annis, R.C. (1987). Racial identity and preference in Native and White Canadian children. *Canadian Journal of Behavioural Science, 19*, 254–65.

Corenblum, B. and Wilson, A.E. (1982). Ethnic preference and identification among Canadian Indian and White children: Replication and extension. *Canadian Journal of Behavioural Science, 14*, 50–9.

Crandall, V.C., Crandall, V.J. and Katkovsky, W. (1965). A social desirability questionnaire. *Journal of Consulting Psychology, 29*, 27–36.

Crooks, R.C. (1970). The effects of an interracial preschool program upon racial preference, knowledge of racial differences, and racial identification. *Journal of Social Issues, 26*, 137–44.

Cross, W.E. (1980). Models of psychological nigrescence: A literature review. In R.L. Jones (ed.), *Black psychology*. New York: Harper and Row, pp. 81–98.

Cross, W.E. (1987). A two-factor theory of Black identity. In J.S. Phinney and M.J. Rotheram (eds.), *Children's ethnic socialization*. Beverley Hills: Sage, 117–33.

Crowne, D.P. and Marlowe, D. (1964). *The approval motive: Studies in evaluative dependence*. New York: Wiley.

Damico, S.B., Bell–Nathaniel A. and Green, C. (1981). Effects of school organizational structure on interracial friendships in middle schools. *Journal of Educational Research, 74*, 388–95.

Davey, A.G. (1983). *Learning to be prejudiced: Growing up in multi-ethnic Britain*. London: Edward Arnold.

Davey A.G. and Mullin, P.N. (1980). Ethnic identification and preference of British primary school children. *Journal of Child Psychology and Psychiatry, 21*, 241–51.

Davidson, F.N. (1976). Ability to respect persons compared to ethnic prejudice in childhood. *Journal of Personality and Social Psychology, 34*, 1256–67.

Doyle, A.B., Beaudet, J. and Aboud, F.E. (1987). Developmental patterns in the flexibility of children's ethnic attitudes. *Journal of Cross-Cultural Psychology*, in press.

Enright, R.D. and Lapsley, D.K. (1981). Judging others who hold opposite beliefs: The development of belief-discrepancy reasoning. *Child Development, 52*, 1053–63.

Epstein, R. and Komorita, S.S. (1966). Childhood prejudice as a function of parental ethnocentrism, punitiveness and outgroup characteristics. *Journal of Personality and Social Psychology, 3*, 259–64.

Epstein, I.M., Krupat, E. and Obudho, C. (1976). Clean is beautiful: Identification and preference as a function of race and cleanliness. *Journal of Social Issues, 32*, 109–18.

Finkelstein, N.W. and Haskins R. (1983). Kindergarten children prefer same-colour peers. *Child Development, 54*, 502–8.

Flavell, J.H. (1977). *Cognitive development*. Englewood Cliffs, N.J.: Prentice-Hall.

Fox, D.J. and Jordan, V.D. (1973). Racial preference and identification of Black, American Chinese, and White children. *Genetic Psychology Monographs, 88*, 229–86.

Friedman, P. (1980). Racial preferences and identification of White elementary schoolchildren. *Contemporary Educational Psychology, 5*, 256–65.

Fu, V.R. and Fogel, S.W. (1982). Prowhite/antiblack bias among southern preschool children. *Psychological Reports, 51*, 1003–6.

Fu, V.R., Hinkle, D.E. and Korslund, M.K. (1983). A developmental study of ethnic self-concept among preadolescent girls. *Journal of Genetic Psychology, 142*, 67–73.

Genesee F., Tucker, G.R. and Lambert, W.E. (1978). The development of ethnic identity and ethnic role-taking skills in children from different school settings. *International Journal of Psychology, 13*, 39–57.

George, D.M. and Hoppe, R.A. (1979). Racial identification, preference, and self-concept. *Journal of Cross-cultural Psychology, 10*, 85–100.

Glasberg, R. and Aboud, F.E. (1981). A developmental perspective on the study of depression: Children's evaluative reactions to sadness. *Developmental Psychology, 17*, 195–202.

Goldstein, C.G., Koopman, E.J. and Goldstein, H.H. (1979). Racial attitudes in young children as a function of interracial contact in the public schools. *American Journal of Orthopsychiatry, 49*, 89–99.

Gottfried, A.W. and Gottfried, A.E. (1974). Influence of social power vs. status envy modeled behaviors on children's preferences for models. *Psychological Reports, 34*, 1147–50.

Greenwald, H.J. and Oppenheim, D.B. (1968). Reported magnitude of self-misidentification among Negro children: Artifact? *Journal of Personality and Social Psychology, 8*, 49–52.

Gregor, A.J. and McPherson, D.A. (1966a). Racial attitudes among White and Negro children in a deep-south standard metropolitan area. *Journal of Social Psychology, 68*, 95–106.

Gregor, A.J. and McPherson, D.A. (1966b). Racial preference and ego-identity among White and Bantu children in the Republic of South Africa. *Genetic Psychology Monographs, 73*, 217–53.

Harter, S. and Pike, R. (1984). The pictorial scale of perceived competence and social acceptance for young children. *Child Development, 55*, 1969–82.

Hewstone, M. and Brown, R. (1986). Contact is not enough: An intergroup perspective on the contact hypothesis. In M. Hewston and R. Brown, *Contact and conflict in intergroup encounters*. Oxford and New York: Blackwell.

Horn, J.L. and Donaldson, G. (1976). On the myth of intellectual decline in adulthood. *American Psychologist, 31*, 701–19.

Hraba, J. (1972). The doll technique: A measure of racial ethnocentrism? *Social Forces, 50*, 522–7.

Hraba, J. and Grant, G. (1970). Black is beautiful: A reexamination of racial preference and identification. *Journal of Personality and Social Psychology, 16*, 398–402.

Hunsberger, B. (1978). Racial awareness and preference of White and Indian Canadian children. *Canadian Journal of Behavioural Science, 10*, 176–9.

Iadicola, P. (1983). Schooling and symbolic violence: The effect of power differences and curriculum factors on Hispanic students' attitudes towards their own ethnicity. *Hispanic Journal of Behavioral Sciences, 5*, 21–43.

Jackson, D.N. and Paunonen, S.V. (1980). Personality structure and assessment. *Annual Review of Psychology, 31,* 503–51.

Johnson, N.B., Middleton, M.R. and Tajfel, H. (1970). The relationship between children's preferences for and knowledge about other nations. *British Journal of Social and Clinical Psychology, 9,* 232–40.

Jones, R.A. and Ashmore, R.D. (1973). The structure of intergroup perception. *Journal of Personality and Social Psychology, 25,* 428–38.

Kalin, R. (1979). Ethnic and multicultural attitudes among children in a Canadian city. *Canadian Ethnic Studies, 11,* 69–81.

Katz, P.A. (1973). Stimulus predifferentiation and modification of children's racial attitudes. *Child Development, 44,* 232–7.

Katz, P.A. (1976). The acquisition of racial attitudes in children. In P.A. Katz (ed.), *Towards the elimination of racism.* New York: Pergamon.

Katz, P.A., Sohn, M. and Zalk, S.R. (1975). Perceptual concomitants of racial attitudes in urban grade-school children. *Developmental Psychology, 11,* 135–44.

Katz, P.A. and Zalk, S.R. (1974). Doll preferences: An index of racial attitudes? *Journal of Educational Psychology, 66,* 663–8.

Katz, P.A. and Zalk, S.R. (1978). Modification of children's racial attitudes. *Developmental Psychology, 14,* 447–61.

Kircher, M. and Furby, L. (1971). Racial preferences in young children. *Child Development, 42,* 2076–8.

Klein, P.S., Levine, E. and Charry, M.M. (1979). Effects of skin color and hair differences on facial choices of kindergarten children. *Journal of Social Psychology, 107,* 287–8.

Kohlberg, L. (1976). Moral stages and moralization: The cognitive–developmental approach. In T. Lickona (ed.), *Moral development and behavior.* New York: Holt, Rinehart and Winston.

Lambert, W.E. and Klineberg, O. (1967). *Children's views of foreign peoples: A cross-national study.* New York: Appleton–Century–Crofts.

Lambert, W.E. and Tucker, G.R. (1972). *Bilingual education of children.* Reading, Mass.: Newbury House.

Lefley, H.P. (1975). Differential self-concept in American Indian children as a function of language and examiner. *Journal of Personality and Social Psychology, 31,* 36–41.

Lerner, R.M. and Buehrig, C.J. (1975). The development of racial attitudes in young Black and White children. *Journal of Genetic Psychology, 127,* 45–54.

Lerner, R.M. and Schroeder, B. (1975). Racial attitudes in young White children: A methodological analysis. *Journal of Genetic Psychology, 127,* 3–12.

LeVine, R.A. and Campbell, D.T. (1972). *Ethnocentrism: Theories of conflict, ethnic attitudes and group behavior.* New York: Wiley.

Likover, B. (1971). The effect of black history on an interracial group of children. *Children, 17,* 177–82.

McGuire, W.J., McGuire, C.V., Child, P. and Fujioka, T. (1978). Salience of ethnicity in the spontaneous self-concept as a function of one's ethnic distinctiveness in the social environment. *Journal of Personality and Social Psychology, 36,* 511–20.

Madge, N.J.H. (1976). Context and the expressed ethnic preferences of infant school children. *Journal of Child Psychology and Psychiatry*, *17*, 337–44.

Marcus, D.E. and Overton, W.F. (1978). The development of cognitive gender constancy and sex role preferences. *Child Development*, *49*, 434–44.

Marsh, A. (1970). Awareness of racial differences in West African and British children. *Race*, *11*, 289–302.

Martin, C.L. and Halverson, C.F. (1981). A schematic processing model of sex-typing and stereotyping in children. *Child Development*, *49*, 1119–34.

Middleton, M.R., Tajfel, H. and Johnson, N.B. (1970). Cognitive and affective aspects of children's national attitudes. *British Journal of Social and Clinical Psychology*, *9*, 122–34.

Milner, D. (1973). Racial identification and preference in Black British children. *European Journal of Social Psychology*, *3*, 281–95.

Moore, C.L. (1976). The racial preference and attitude of preschool Black children. *Journal of Genetic Psychology*, *129*, 37–44.

Morland, J.K. (1966). A comparison of race awareness in Northern and Southern children. *American Journal of Orthopsychiatry*, *36*, 22–31.

Morland, J.K. and Hwang, C.H. (1981). Racial/ethnic identity of preschool children. *Journal of Cross-Cultural Psychology*, *12*, 409–24.

Morland, J.K. and Suthers, E. (1980). Racial attitudes of children: Perspectives on the structural-normative theory of prejudice. *Phylon*, 267–75.

Moscovici, S. and Paicheler, G. (1978). Social comparison and social recognition: Two complementary processes of identification. In H. Tajfel (ed.), *Differentiation between social groups*. New York: Academic Press.

Mosher, D.L. and Scodel, A. (1960). Relationships between enthnocentrism in children and the ethnocentrism and authoritarian rearing practices of their mothers. *Child Development*, *31*, 369–76.

Newman, M.A., Liss, M.B. and Sherman, F. (1983). Ethnic awareness in children: Not a unitary concept. *Journal of Genetic Psychology*, *143*, 103–12.

Novak, T.A. and Richman, C.L. (1980). The effects of stimulus variability on overgeneralization and overdiscrimination errors in children and adults. *Child Development*, *51*, 55–60.

Orive, R. and Gerard, H.B. (1975). Social contact of minority parents and their children's acceptance by classmates. *Sociometry*, *38*, 518–24.

Pettigrew, T.F. (1967). Social evaluation theory: Convergences and applications. *Nebraska Symposium of Motivation*, *15*, 241–318.

Pettigrew, T.F. (1986). The intergroup contact hypothesis reconsidered. In M. Hewston and R. Brown (eds.), *Contact and conflict in intergroup encounters*. Oxford and New York: Blackwell.

Piaget, J. (1932). *The moral judgement of the child*. London: Kegan Paul.

Piaget, J. and Weil, A.M. (1951). The development in children of the idea of the homeland and of relations to other countries. *International Social Science Journal*, *3*, 561–78.

Ramsey, P.G. (1987). Young children's thinking about ethnic differences. In J.S. Phinney and M.J. Rotheram (eds.), *Children's ethnic socialization*. Beverly Hills: Sage.

Renninger, C.A. and Williams, J.E. (1966). Black-white color connotations and racial awareness in preschool children. *Perceptual and Motor Skills, 22*, 771–85.

Rice, A.S., Ruiz, R.A. and Padilla, A.M. (1974). Person perception, self-identity, and ethnic group preference in Anglo, Black, and Chicano preschool and third-grade children. *Journal of Cross-Cultural Psychology, 5*, 100–8.

Roberts, A., Moseley, K. and Chamberlain, M. (1975). Age differences in racial self-identity of young black girls. *Psychological Reports, 37*, 1263–6.

Rohrer, G.K. (1977). Racial and ethnic identification and preference in young children. *Young Children, 32*, 24-33.

Rosenbaum, M.E. (1986). The repulsion hypothesis: On the nondevelopment of relationships. *Journal of Personality and Social Psychology, 51*, 1156–66.

Rosenberg, M. (1979). *Conceiving the self*. New York: Basic Books.

Rosenberg, M. and Simmons, R.G. (1971). *Black and White self-esteem: The urban school child*. Washington: American Sociological Association.

Rosenthal, B.G. (1974). Development of self-identification in relation to attitudes toward the self in the Chippewa Indians. *Genetic Psychology Monographs, 90*, 43–141.

Rothbart, M. (1976). Achieving racial equality: An analysis of resistance to social reform. In P.A. Katz (ed.), *Towards the elimination of racism*. New York: Pergamon Press, pp. 341–75.

Rothbart, M., Fulero, S., Jensen, C., Howard, J. and Birrell, P. (1978). From individual to group impressions: Availability heuristics in stereotype formation. *Journal of Experimental Social Psychology, 14*, 237–55.

St John, N.H. and Lewis, R.G. (1975). Race and the social structure of the elementary classroom. *Sociology of Education, 48*, 346–68.

Schofield, J.W. (1978). An exploratory study of the Draw-a-Person as a measure of racial identity. *Perceptual and Motor Skills, 46*, 311–21.

Schofield, J.W. (1986). Black–white contact in desegregated schools. In M. Hewstone and R. Brown, *Contact and conflict in intergroup encounters*. Oxford and New York: Blackwell, pp. 79–92.

Schofield, J.W. and Francis, W.D. (1982). An observational study of peer interaction in racially mixed 'accelerated' classrooms. *Journal of Educational Psychology, 74*, 722–32.

Sedlak, A.J. and Kurtz, S.T. (1982). A review of children's use of causal inference principles. *Child Development, 52*, 759–84.

Selman, R.L. (1980). *The growth of interpersonal understanding: Developmental and clinical analyses*. New York: Academic.

Semaj, L. (1980). The development of racial evaluation and preference: A cognitive approach. *Journal of Black Psychology, 6*, 59–79.

Sherif, M. and Sherif, C.W. (1969). *Social psychology*. New York: Harper and Row.

Simon, R.J. (1974). An assessment of racial awareness, preference and self-identity among White and adopted non-White children. *Social Problems, 22*, 43–57.

Singleton, L.C. and Asher, S.R. (1979). Racial integration and children's peer preferences: An investigation of developmental and cohort differences. *Child Development, 50,* 936–41.

Slaby, R.G. and Frey, K.S. (1975). Development of gender constancy and selective attention to same-sex models. *Child Development, 46,* 849–56.

Spencer, M.B. (1982). Personal and group identity of black children: An alternative synthesis. *Genetic Psychology Monographs, 106,* 59–84.

Spencer, M.B. (1983). Children's cultural values and parental rearing strategies. *Developmental Review, 3,* 351–70.

Stephan, W.G. (1978). School desegregation: An evaluation of predictions made in Brown vs. Board of Education. *Psychological Bulletin, 85,* 217–38.

Stephan, W.G. and Rosenfield, D. (1979). Black self-rejection: Another look. *Journal of Educational Psychology, 71,* 708–16.

Stevenson, H.W. and Stewart, E.C. (1958). A developmental study of racial awareness in young children. *Child Development, 29,* 399–409.

Tajfel, H. (1978). Social categorization, social identity and social comparison. In H. Tajfel (ed.), *Differentiation between social groups.* New York: Academic Press, pp. 61–98.

Tajfel, H., Jahoda, G., Nemeth, C., Rim, Y. and Johnson, N.B. (1972). The devaluation by children of their own national and ethnic group: Two case studies. *British Journal of Social and Clincial Psychology, 11,* 235–43.

Tajfel, H., Nemeth, C., Jahoda, G., Campbell, J.D. and Johnson, N.B. (1970). The development of children's preferences for their own country: A cross-national study. *International Journal of Psychology, 5,* 245–53.

Tracy, J.J. and Cross, H.J. (1973). Antecedents of shift in moral judgment. *Journal of Personality and Social Psychology, 26,* 238–44.

Turner, J.C. (1978). Social categorization and social discrimination in the minimal group paradigm. In H. Tajfel (ed.), *Differentiation between social groups.* New York: Academic Press, pp. 101–40.

Vaughan, G.M. (1963). Concept formation and the development of ethnic awareness. *Journal of Genetic Psychology, 103,* 93–103.

Vaughan, G.M. (1964). The development of ethnic attitudes in New Zealand school children. *Genetic Psychology Monographs, 70,* 135–75.

Vaughan, G.M. (1978). Social categorization and intergroup behaviour in children. In H. Tajfel (ed.), *Differentiation between social groups.* New York: Academic Press, pp. 339–60.

Vaughan, G.M. (1987). A social psychological model of ethnic identity. In J.S. Phinney and M.J. Rotheram (eds.), *Children's ethnic socialization.* Beverly Hills: Sage, pp. 73–91.

Verna, G.B. (1981). Use of a free-response task to measure children's race preferences, *Journal of Genetic Psychology, 138,* 87–93.

Verna, G.B. (1982). A study of the nature of children's race preferences using a modified conflict paradigm. *Child Development, 53,* 437–45.

Ward, S.H. and Braun, J. (1972). Self-esteem and racial preference in Black children. *American Journal of Orthopsychiatry, 42,* 644–7.

Weiland, A. and Coughlin, R. (1979). Self-identification and preferences: A comparison of White and Mexican–American first and third graders. *Journal of Cross-Cultural Psychology, 10*, 356–65.

Weinheimer, S. (1972). Egocentrism and social influence in children. *Child Development, 43*, 567–78.

Werner, N.E. and Idella, M.E. (1968). Perception of prejudice in Mexican–American preschool children. *Perceptual and Motor Skills, 27*, 1039–46.

Wetherell, M. (1982). Cross-cultural studies of minimal groups: Implications for the social identity theory of intergroup relations. In H. Tajfel (ed.), *Social identity and intergroup relations*. Cambridge: Cambridge University Press.

Whitley, B.E., Schofield, J.W. and Snyder, H.N. (1984). Peer preferences in a desegregated school: A round robin analysis. *Journal of Personality and Social Psychology, 46*, 799–810.

Williams, J.E., Best, D.L. and Boswell, D.A. (1975). The measurement of children's racial attitudes in the early school years. *Child Development, 46*, 494–500.

Williams, J.E. and Morland, J.K. (1976). *Race, color, and the young child*. Chapel Hill: University of North Carolina Press.

Womack, W.M. and Fulton, W. (1981). Transracial adoption and the Black preschool child. *Journal of the American Academy of Child Psychiatry, 20*, 712–24.

Zajonc, R.B. (1980). Feeling and thinking: Preferences need no inferences. *American Psychologist, 35*, 151–75.

Zanna, M.P. and Rempel, J.K. (in press). Attitudes: A new look at an old concept. In D. Bar-Tal and A. Kruglanski (eds), *The social psychology of knowledge*. Cambridge: Cambridge University Press.

Zinser, O., Rich, M.C. and Bailey, R.C. (1981). Sharing behavior and racial preference in children. *Motivation and Emotion, 5*, 179–87.

Author Index

Subject Index

affective processes 23–4, 116–19
aggression 20, 65
anger 20, 21
Asian children
    attitudes toward ingroup 42–3
    awareness, ethnic 47, 49
    prejudice 42–3
    self-identification, ethnic 55
assessment techniques *see*
    measurement
attachment 117–18
attitude development
    causal factors 74–100
    empirical findings 28–43
    of majority children 29–36
    of minority children 37–43
    theories of 17–27, 71, 74, 115–27
attitudes toward ingroup
    causal factors 74–100
    development of 34–43
    of majority children 34–46
    measurement 8–12
    of minority children 19, 37–43, 68,
      75
authoritarian personality 20–2, 90–2,
    102
awareness, ethnic
    definition of 6–8
    development of 46–51
    of majority children 46–51
    measurement 12–14
    of minority children 46–51
    of own group *see* self-identification

relation to prejudice 7, 45

Black children
    attitudes toward ingroup 37–42, 82,
      89–90
    awareness, ethic 46–7, 49
    prejudice 37–42
    self-identification, ethnic 15, 53–5,
      56–7, 123

categorization 7, 13–14, 19, 25, 48–9,
    56, 76–7, 79, 85
Chicano children *see* Hispanic children
child-rearing practices 20–1, 90–2
Chinese children *see* Asian children
cognitive processes 7
    cognitive development 22–6, 104–14
    ethnic cognitions 24, 87, 105–14
    relation to prejudice 119–21
cohort effects 69–70
conflict 20, 65, 66–7
conformity 26, 67
conservation 104, 105, 114
constancy, ethnic 8, 14–15, 49–51,
    113–14
contact, ethnic 65, 81–5
continuous rating scales 9–10, 33, 36,
    68

differentiation 4
    between-groups 13, 23
    within-group 13, 23, 26
discrimination 4